# Enterprise Architecture
## A Practitioner's Handbook

–Cover Art–

Galileo Galilei
The work of art itself is in the public domain and was sourced from Wikimedia commons.

The Father of Modern Science, Galileo was a supreme polymath, a master of many disciplines: astronomer, physicist, engineer, philosopher, and mathematician.

Now is the time for enterprise architects to become the new polymaths for today.

# Enterprise Architecture
## A Practitioner's Handbook

*Gopala Krishna Behara*
*Sameer S. Paradkar*

**MK**
Meghan-Kiffer Press
Tampa, Florida, USA
www.mkpress.com
*Innovation at the Intersection of Business and Technology*

ISBN 10: 0-929652-56-8 ISBN 13: 978-0-929652-56-6

Published by Meghan-Kiffer Press
   310 East Fern Street — Suite G
   Tampa, FL 33604 USA

Company and product names mentioned herein are the trademarks or registered trademarks of their respective owners.

Meghan-Kiffer books are available at special quantity discounts for corporate education and training use. For more information write Special Sales, Meghan-Kiffer Press, Suite G, 310 East Fern Street, Tampa, Florida 33604 or email orders@mkpress.com

Meghan-Kiffer Press
Tampa, Florida, USA
*Innovation at the Intersection of Business and Technology*

Printed in the United States of America.    SAN 249-7980
Editor: Marilyn Krause Babb
MK Printing 10 9 8 7 6 5 4 3 2 1

# Table of Contents

# Preface

At the epicenter of any transformation project, one must first have a clear picture of the current state. This reference guide provides a step-by-step approach and methodology to scan and document the present state, as indicated by CIOs and IT Directors who struggle with transformation and IT budgetary challenges on a daily basis. Without understanding the present situation, the current state, we cannot accurately capture the magnitude of issues, challenges and pain points as we embark on the journey to modernize and transform the business and technology landscapes. I hope you will use this reference guide to benchmark where your enterprise is today and to devise intelligent, cost-saving alternatives to modernize and transform the landscape for the future.

This reference guide consolidates the experience of many projects and programs with customers, and insights from many hours of intense discussions with experts from client companies and consultancies. The book takes a holistic view of the Enterprise Architecture Transformation, while also giving specific guidelines on how to establish and roll out future-state Enterprise Architecture based on the methodology and approach documented in this reference guide.

# Acknowledgements

We thank our discussion partners, reviewers and supporters, whose valuable comments and feedback have greatly contributed to this book. We look forward to your feedback and valuable inputs on an on-going basis.

We would like to thank our family members and friends for their encouragement and constant support during the long hours and lost weekends required to create this book.

# 1. Introduction

IT has always been at the forefront of innovation. New applications accelerate an organization's growth, automate key business processes and also provide competitive edge. But the cutting-edge systems of yesterday become legacy systems of today. These legacy applications still support core business processes and comprise the majority of an organization's application assets. However, they are often written in outdated development languages and run on platforms and infrastructure that cannot integrate and scale up based on the organization's business needs.

Organizations often chose to write custom applications rather than purchase commercial off-the-shelf COTS systems. The larger and more profitable the organization, the bigger are its IT teams, creating a need for customized applications tailored to meet the organization's business needs. But as organizations grow, develop new products, merge and acquire new business units, they begin to lose control of the rapidly growing landscape of custom built applications and databases. Unable to cope with the potential risks of retiring legacy systems, and replace them with new, consolidated applications, many organizations have chosen to maintain and support their original legacy systems. Keeping these systems up and running requires dedicated teams with skill sets that are hard to find. Most organizations do not have a clear strategy for retiring legacy applications and continue to spend a fortune of their IT budgets just keeping the lights on, supporting outdated, redundant and sometimes entirely obsolete systems.

Importantly the sprawled application landscape leaves almost no room for innovation and hinders business agility. Lack of centralized reporting systems can cause organizations to make critical mistakes in taking product inventory, tracking shipments or processing payments. And with many redundant systems running similar transactions, it becomes very difficult to pinpoint the root cause of a given problem.

One more common issue with application growth is an exponential increase in data size. Even the simplest IT systems are capable of generating large quantities of data such as transaction records, customer information and shipping details. Without proper archiving methods, stored data can grow exponentially.

### *Challenges Faced by CxOs*

An enterprise's application landscape includes more applications than the business needs. This increases operating expenses and diverts attention from the important goals of innovation and growth. To avoid such a drain on resources, a top priority of the CIO must be to develop a closer alignment of business goals and IT.

CIO/CTO needs to simultaneously manage the technology backbone of the business and also plan for future growth while constantly adjusting to unprecedented changes in technology. They also must spearhead the direction and implementation of IT throughout their organization, acting as change management leaders.

The CIO position is a mix of two different roles. One covers operational requirements, ensuring that systems, applications and data centers are up and running, managing security and disaster recovery and ensuring rapid responses to queries. The other role is that of a change agent who uncovers methods for empowering strategic opportunities within the company.

To achieve an effective realignment, an enterprise needs to review its current application landscape and create long-term modernization strategies as explained in the later sections of this book:

- Managing interdependencies and connections that exist within and between business and IT structures
- Identifying potential for optimization in IT
- Determining interdependencies and the impact of changes in IT and business
- Building the EA in compliance with standards, processes and frameworks
- Effectively steering the future development of the EA
- Making visible the contribution of IT to the business success of the enterprise
- Building EA that supports the organizational vision and address the IT strategy for the next 3-5 years
- Analyzing and appraising the potential impact of organizational restructuring
- IT and business alignment
- Compliance and regulatory oversight
- Enterprise Resilience to guard against disruptions
- Budget Reductions
- Managing the ever increasing pace of business change
- Managing IT in the current economic climate
- The interplay between IT strategy and shorter term tactics are illustrated in the following table.

| Rank | CIO Technology Priorities - 2015 |
| --- | --- |
| 1 | Analytics and Business Intelligence |
| 2 | Infrastructure & Data Centre |
| 3 | Cloud |
| 4 | ERP |
| 5 | Mobile |
| 6 | Digitalization/Digital Marketing |
| 7 | Security |
| 8 | Networking Voice Datacomm |
| 9 | CRM |
| 10 | Industry Specific Application |
| 11 | Legacy Modernization |
| 12 | Enterprise Application |

*CIO Priorities – Gartner 2015*

### Software Architecture

Software Architecture is the process of defining a structured solution that meets all of the requirements of a business, while optimizing common quality attributes such as performance, scalability, and security. It involves a series of decisions based on a wide range of factors and each of these decisions can have considerable impact on the NFRs including, but not limited to quality, performance, maintainability and overall success of the application. In Software Architecture in Practice (2nd edition), Bass, Clements, and Kazman define software architecture as follows: "The software architecture of a program or computing system is the structure or structures of the system, which comprise software elements, the externally visible properties of those elements, and the relationships among them. Architecture is concerned with the public side of interfaces not the private details of elements. Details having to do solely with internal implementation are not architectural."

### *Enterprise Architecture*

Enterprise Architecture (EA) in an organization is often defined as the organizing logic for business processes and infrastructure. The primary purpose of creating enterprise architecture is to ensure that business strategy and IT are aligned. Enterprise architecture should make it possible for an organization to achieve traceability from the business strategy down to the technology used to implement that strategy.

The practice of enterprise architecture has come to include activities that help decision makers understand, analyze, optimize, justify and communicate a given structure, including relationships between business entities and software components. EA practice looks at the current state (as-is architecture) to help build and navigate the future state (to-be architecture) of the organization. EA activities establish a roadmap to reach the future state.

Enterprise architecture pulls together the pockets of information scattered across the organization's various business units and service lines, creating a unified picture that highlights how the information is networked along with its interdependencies. This big picture view is invaluable for every enterprise in underpinning a range of IT management tasks. In essence the enterprise architecture is the basis for strategic management of the application landscape.

## EA means architecting the enterprise for change

### Enterprise Architecture Is

A Discipline for proactively and holistically leading enterprise responses to disruptive forces by identifying and analyzing the execution of change towards desired business vision and outcomes

### EA Delivers Value By

Presenting business & IT leaders with signature ready recommendations for adjusting policies and projects to achieve target business outcomes that capitalize on relevant business disruptions

### EA is Used

To steer decision making towards the evolution of the future state architecture

### Scope of Enterprise Architecture Includes

The people, processes, information and technology of the enterprise, and their relationships to one another and to the external environment

*EA Definition*

### *Without Enterprise Architecture*

The challenges faced by organizations in the absence of Enterprise Architecture are the weak linkages between intent and focus regarding corporate strategy, governance, and technology initiatives. To wit:

**Strategy**

- No link to business strategic planning and budget process
- Slow and ineffective decision-making

- Inability to rapidly respond to changes driven by business challenges
- Lack of focus on enterprise requirements
- Lack of common direction and synergies
- Blind focus on the art or language of EA rather than the path to desired outcomes
- Incomplete process closure (aka lack of effective supervisory enforcement) of the current and future target Enterprise Architecture vision
- Lack of flexibility to alter course or change tools as needed when the focus is on the individual strategy rather than corporate strategy

**Governance**
- Inability to predict impacts of future changes
- Confusing "IT Architecture" With "Enterprise Architecture"
- Lack of governance
- Strict following of EA frameworks
- "Ivory Tower" approach
- Lack of communication and feedback
- Limiting the EA team to IT resources
- Lack of performance measures
- No measurement criteria for EA metrics
- Picking a tool before understanding your business needs, or alternately before vetting the tech support and training the tool vendor provides

**Technology**
- Increased gaps and architecture conflicts
- Lack of commonality and consistency due to the absence of standards
- Dilution and dissipation of critical information and knowledge of the deployed solutions
- Rigidity, redundancy and lack of scalability and flexibility in the deployed solutions

- Over-standardization
- Non-adoption of Next Generation Technologies
- Lack of integration, compatibility and interoperability between applications
- Complex, fragile and costly interfaces between incongruent application

### *Architecture Phases*

A typical enterprise architecture engagement consists of three phases as listed below:

- Planning Phase
- Definition Phase
- Governance Phase

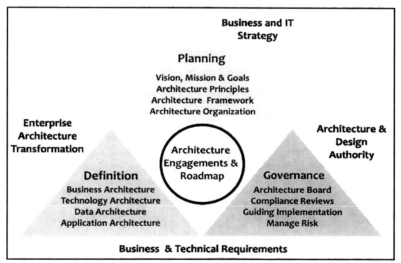

*EA Phases*

## Planning Phase

The planning phase includes establishing the architecture approach, principles, scope, vision, mission and goals.

Vision and Mission statements play an important role in strategy development by providing vehicles to

generate and screen strategic options. They also provide organizational identity and understanding of
business directions.

| Phase | Definition | Description |
|---|---|---|
| **Vision** | Dream or Picture to be achieved | Created by consensus. Forms mental image of future to which people can align. Describes something possible, not necessarily predictable. Provides direction and focus. |
| *e.g. Offer an affordable Solution to health care* | | |
| **Mission** | Statement of business | States the business reason for the organization's existence. Defines current and future business in terms of product, score, customer, reason, market price. |
| *Strives to support education improvements by providing software tools* | | |
| **Goals** | Results to be achieved | Describes ideal states to be achieved at some future time. Definition consistent with and related directly to vision and mission. Guides everyday decisions and actions. |
| *e.g. Reduce overall budget costs by 10% by 20xx* | | |
| **Objective** | Plans to achieve the desired results | Focuses on critical organization issues and milestones. Describes activities to be accomplished to achieve goals. Measurable in terms of whether or not goals are achieved. |

*Vision, Mission and Goals*

**Definition Phase**

The definition phase includes the creation of architecture artifacts by iterating through Business, Information Systems, and Technology Architectures phases.

Enterprise architecture seeks to build a bridge between business requirements and technical require-

ments by understanding use cases and business scenarios, and then finding ways to implement those use cases through software. The goal of architecture is to identify the requirements that affect the structure of software applications. Good architecture reduces the business risks associated with building a technical solution. A good design is agile enough to handle the natural drift that will occur over time in hardware and software technology, as well as in user scenarios and business requirements. An architect must analyze and drive the architectural decisions, the inherent tradeoffs between quality attributes (such as performance and security), and the tradeoffs required to address user, system, and business requirements.

Embracing all the major business and IT structures as well as the associations that exist between them, enterprise architecture creates a helicopter view of the entire organization. It serves as a basis for describing the business objectives and IT directives, as well as the connections between them, thus creating a common language bridging the gap between business and IT.

However, only when the enterprise has a complete picture of the landscape and an awareness of its components and the links (and gaps) between them can it make appropriate decisions for business.

**EA Domains**

The best practice enterprise architecture is essentially comprised of a range of sub-architectures, each of which examines IT from a different perspective. The work is begun with an effort to systematically describe the IT structures from various perspectives and define each in its own model for later comparison and value mapping.

Each sub-architecture stakes out specific rules for how the constituent entities should be modeled. For instance, the business architecture defines rules for the business landscape model: how business processes are to be described and which business process levels are to be taken into consideration.

We differentiate between the following sub-architectures, or domains. The following diagram depicts the scope of various domains that are part of the architecture.

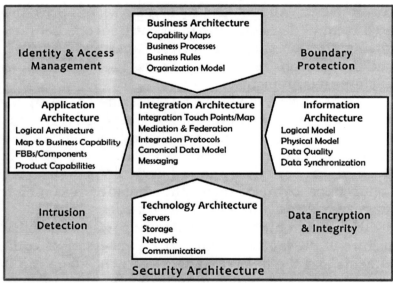

*EA Domains*

## Governance Phase

Architecture Governance is the practice and orientation by which enterprise architectures and other architectures are monitored, managed and controlled. Architecture Governance is required to ensure the principles of Enterprise Architecture are applied to both systems architecture and design of the underlying information systems. In plain language, governance supports completion of the mission. It also ensures organizations collaboratively meet business and IT objectives and standards. Architecture Governance enables effective alignment of business and information technology, manages risk by reducing probability of failures in transformation projects, and incorporates elements of cost effectiveness and value.

### *Benefits of Enterprise Architecture*

Enterprise Architecture is not a one-time event, nor limited to specific projects or business units. EA is an on-going, iterative process that provides a powerful structure to define, refine, and interconnect. The end goal of EA is agility.

The purpose of enterprise architecture is to optimize the often fragmented legacy of business processes, both manual and automated, into an integrated environment that is responsive to change and supportive to the delivery of the business strategy. Effective management of information through IT is a key factor to business success and a means to achieving competitive advantage. Enterprise Architecture addresses this need, by providing a strategic context for the evolution of IT systems in response to the constantly changing demands of the business environment.

A simplified list of EA benefits includes:

- A common vision of the future shared by business and IT; business aware of IT and vice-versa
- Guidance in the selection, creation and implementation of solutions driven by business requirements
- Support for the various enterprise business lines through improved information sharing – provides a plan for the integration of information and services at the design level across business lines

- A means to control growing complexities of technology by setting enterprise-wide, leverage-able standards for information technology
- Defines an approach for the evaluation, consideration and assimilation of new and emerging technology innovations to meet business requirements

The advantages that result from a good enterprise architecture can bring important benefits, including:

**Technology Benefits of EA**

- Lower software development, support, and maintenance costs
- Increased portability of applications
- Improved interoperability and easier system and network management
- Improved ability to address critical enterprise-wide issues, such as security
- Easier upgrade and exchange of system components
- Reduced complexity in IT infrastructure
- Generates portfolio of IT assets
- Enables what-if analysis
- Helps in IT Asset Rationalization
- Improves sharing of services

**Business Benefits of EA**

- Highly optimized and flexible processes (Business & IT)
- Ability to integrate seamlessly with systems within the enterprise and among partners
- Highly optimized and shared IT infrastructure
- Loosely coupled systems to quickly respond to new processes or a new product or a new channel – Business value generation

- Well mapping of business processes to application to information to technology
- Strict adherence to regulatory and compliance factors
- Maximum return on investment in existing IT infrastructure
- The flexibility to make, buy, or out-source IT solutions
- Reduced overall risk in new investment, and the costs of IT ownership
- Buying decisions are made simpler, because the information governing procurement is readily available in a coherent plan
- The procurement process is faster, maximizing procurement speed and flexibility without sacrificing architectural coherence
- The ability to procure heterogeneous, multi-vendor open systems
- Promotes better planning and decision making
- Ensures Alignment of Technology with Business Drivers
- Improves communication among the Business and IT units
- Improves selection of future IT investments
- Reduces Total Cost of Ownership (TCO)

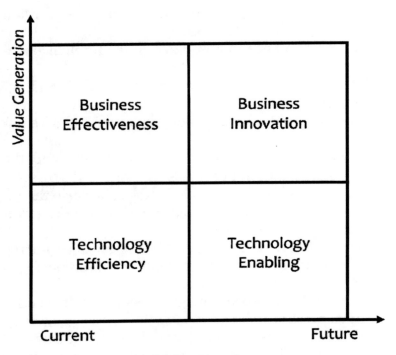

*EA Value Quadrant*

## *Summary*

Today's IT organizations are carrying a heavy burden of applications that are not delivering full value to the business. Rationalization and modernization engagements are needed to simplify the functionality of existing applications and to reduce the amount of old technology thus removing inefficiencies. Companies that have more applications than the business needs are forced to spend valuable IT resources on supporting obsolete systems and thereby lose competitive edge. Enterprise Architecture provides a stable plan for interconnecting business and its technology in an agile and functional way.

# 2. EA Transformation

EA transformation is a discipline where by the application landscape is transformed from the landscape of today (current state) to a future-state strategic landscape supporting business goals and objectives of an enterprise. The transformation journey involves running workshops to understand the issues, challenges, pain areas and gaps in the current landscape. The transformation journey also involves recommending a roadmap to the customer in terms of transitioning from current state to the future state generally recommended using the phased approach as against a big bang approach.

Most CIOs realize that large-scale modernization projects are needed to simplify the functionality of existing applications, to reduce the amount of old technology and to bring new, more effective applications into the business. The mission-critical applications implemented using outdated technology must be revised and updated to increase efficiency.

Despite the challenges, the CIO's outlook on the application lifecycle is beginning to change. Instead of simply building custom IT solutions to solve today's specific problems, IT management is committed to bringing in more standardized, scalable and maintainable offerings. A growing number of IT executives are treating application retirement as an essential step in the lifecycle, and they are adopting new practices for reviewing and modernizing their application landscapes. Only with such a true lifecycle approach can companies maintain a healthy portfolio and ensure productivity, application quality, and optimal business alignment.

As budgets become more constricted, the focus of application strategy shifts from innovation to cost cutting. There was adequate funding before the economic downturn for both "keeping the lights on" and finding room for innovation; today's economic climate clearly highlights new limitations in this area. The resources to support growth and new development, therefore, must now be found within the IT organization itself. By creatively modernizing and rationalizing the application portfolio, IT can derive the needed extra funds. But application rationalization is not an easy task. Cost is a key barrier to all modernization initiatives, and it is often difficult to demonstrate a rapid enough Return on Investment (ROI) to get the management buy in.

### Why EA Transformation

The IT department develops solutions without regard for what will happen when these applications reach the end of their life. Let this sink in for a moment. IT personnel have been trained to deploy and maintain – it has never been their domain to end a lifecycle. In fact, if you can think like an IT technician, you could see how they might look at ending a software solution as a threat to their job security. Software Engineers build applications for specific business processes, patch functionality, periodically upgrading these systems, and managing the multitude of redundant applications and large amounts of data that comes with each merger or acquisition. It is an admirable task, but without proper leadership from above the payoffs can be short lived. This chaotic sprawl causes serious problems. Like an old city with narrow streets and outdated infrastructure desperately trying to provide modern amenities to its fast-growing population, IT struggles to deliver value to the business.

Lack of convincing business cases and coherent strategies, poorly defined architectural alignment, and inconsistent and unreliable application intelligence can significantly hinder any effort to bring order to chaos. CIOs can apply multiple strategies to modernize and rationalize their applications, including sustaining, extending, remediating, migrating, replacing, consolidating, rewriting and retiring. The question is which strategy is the best for a given situation that results in timely realization of ROI to support the near-term business goals. However, many CIOs find it difficult to get support and business buy in for such initiatives.

Today's CIOs are spending too much valuable time, effort and budget on their sprawling application landscape. They struggle to find resources to support innovations and value-driven business initiatives. The top priority for the CIO is to rationalize and modernize the application portfolio to increase productivity, flexibility, adaptability and manageability and better align IT with the business.

Let's now explore the benefits of a transformation in the enterprise architecture, and the simple and yet profound changes a maturing EA approach will provide.

### Benefits of EA Transformation

The following are the key benefits of EA transformation:

- *Create Value for the Business* e.g. improving efficiencies
- *Cut Overall Cost for the Business*, e.g. decommissioning, data archiving, cloud computing
- *Improve Productivity,* e.g. removing inefficiencies, removing excel spread sheets based reporting, incorporating Service Management via ITIL processes

- *Innovate New Application and Services,* e.g. Leveraging competitive advantage of social business
- *Increase Quality of Application,* e.g. standardization and simplification, usage of frameworks
- *Improve Flexibility of IT Systems,* e.g. IT can deliver more value to business
- Create Better IT and Business Alignment
- *Improve Efficiency of IT Systems,* e.g. automating processes or removing manual intervention

### *Enterprise Architecture Maturity*

Many organizations know that they need to improve their Business and IT alignment in order to successfully manage change, but don't know how. Such organizations typically either spend very little on process improvement, because they are unsure how best to proceed; or spend a lot, on a number of parallel and unfocused efforts, to little or no avail.

An evaluation of the Enterprise practices against the model — called an "assessment" — determines the level at which the organization currently stands. It indicates the organization's maturity in the area concerned, and the practices on which the organization needs to focus in order to see the greatest improvement and the highest return on investment. As the Enterprise Architecture (EA) matures the predictability, process controls and effectiveness also increases.

EA progresses in maturity will benefit the organization in the following ways:
- Promote Strategic Initiatives
- Reduced software and data redundancy
- Enhanced enterprise information sharing
- Reduced information systems complexity
- Better alignment of business strategy and system development
- Greater reliability at implementations and updates

28

- Reduced dependency on key resources
- Improved accuracy in scheduling software development and implementation
- More accurate forecasting of development and support costs
- More efficient deployment of technology solutions
- Greater ability to set realistic goals
- Increased traceability

## Maturity Assessment

The main hurdles of the Enterprise Architecture of the Organization are:

- Declarations of business mission, vision, goals, strategy
- Technology and organizational silos prevent the implementation of rapid changes
- Processes not working optimally results in unnecessary expense, customer dissatisfaction and churn
- Business process problems or desired process improvements
- Not possible to monitor end to end process and measure the results
- Difficulty of aligning business needs with IT capabilities

Business Architecture forms the important part in the context of EA. It helps IT to support the business better, cheaper and faster. As part of the EA assessment and EA definition, we need to understand and to define business goals, business strategy, business plans, or initiating business process re-engineering.

Development of the Enterprise Architecture is an ongoing process and cannot be delivered overnight. The establishment an EA is critical because it provides the rules and definition necessary for the integration of information and services at the operational level across enterprise boundaries. An organization must work patiently to nurture and improve its Enterprise Architecture Program until architectural processes and standards become second nature and the Architecture Framework and the Architecture Blueprint become self-renewing.

## EA Maturity Assessment Framework

An EA Maturity Assessment framework comprises a maturity model with different maturity levels and a set of elements which are to be assessed, and a methodology and toolkit for assessment (questionnaires, tools, etc.). The final outcome is a detailed assessment report which describes the maturity of the enterprise as a whole, as well as the maturity against each of the architectural elements. The key components of this framework are depicted below:

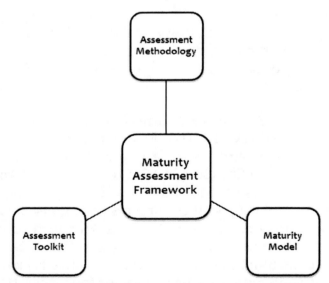

*EA Maturity Assessment Framework*

Enterprise Architecture Maturity Model (EAMM) is used to conduct the Maturity assessment. EAMM provides the framework that represents the key components of a productive enterprise architecture process. The goal is to enhance the overall success of enterprise architecture by identifying weak areas and providing a defined evolutionary path to improving the overall architecture process. The EAMM comprises the following: Architecture Elements, Enterprise Maturity Levels, and a Maturity Score Card

**Enterprise Architecture Element**

Based on Industry Standards and our consulting experience, the following architecture elements are identified and are to be assessed as part of the EA maturity assessment methodology,

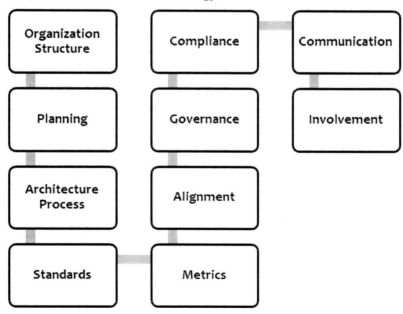

A brief description of each element follows:

**Organization Structure:** This element covers the organization structure that exists for the EA program – roles and responsibilities of team members and their skill sets with respect to Enterprise Architecture.

**Planning:** Planning ensures the program is managed to assure the goals for implementation are realistic and achievable and the program is kept within scope. It also indicates whether a clear vision exists for business architecture development within the enterprise.

**Architecture Process:** This element indicates whether there is any process in place for architecture development and how effectively is it followed.

**Alignment:** This element indicates whether the activities of the IT/Architecture teams are aligned with the organization's business goals and objectives. It indicates whether senior IT management is actively involved with business teams in the decision making process.

**Governance:** Architecture governance is the practice and orientation by which enterprise architectures and other architectures are managed and controlled at an enterprise-wide level.

**Compliance:** Architecture Compliance review is a scrutiny of the compliance of a specific project against established architectural criteria and business objectives.

**Standards:** It covers the processes, guidelines, templates and forms used by those involved in the process of architecture development.

**Involvement:** Involvement must be part of an EA Program. Without the support of managers and employees who are expected to utilize and follow the defined process, the program is sure to fail. Involvement addresses the ability of the various entities (internal or external to the organization) to coordinate their efforts to the greatest benefit of the organization.

**Metrics:** This element indicates EA maturity in terms of measurement and monitoring of EA activities and efforts. It indicates if the results of EA activities are being captured and measured and the benefits of the EA program have been quantified.

**Architecture Communication:** Communication is the element that ensures standards and processes are established and readily available to team members for reference and use. As an organization changes and programs evolve the continued communication ensures the EA program remains vital and operates optimally.

**Enterprise Maturity Levels**

The Enterprise Architecture Maturity Model, depicted below and in the following sections reflect the phases an organization will witness as their architecture program matures. The model follows the path of an organization as their enterprise architecture program matures, and sets benchmarks to measure the performance and path that is a natural progression in the development of enterprise architecture.

In the following sections, each of the levels of the Enterprise Architecture Maturity Model is defined. Each level contains statements that are indicative of an EA Program at that level.

| Level | Description |
|---|---|
| Level 0:<br>No EA | There is not a documented architectural framework in place at this level of maturity. While solutions are developed and implemented, this is done with no recognized standards or base practices. |
| Level 1:<br>Initial | The base architecture framework and standards have been defined and are typically performed informally. Organizations with an Enterprise Architecture framework at this level are still dependent on the knowledge of individual contributors. |
| Level 2:<br>Under<br>Development | The vision, principles, base architecture and standards have been identified and are being tracked and verified. At this point in the maturity program processes are repeatable and reusable. Templates are starting to be developed. |
| Level 3:<br>Defined | The enterprise architecture framework is well defined using approved standard and/or customized versions of the templates. Processes are documented across the organization. Performance metrics are being tracked and monitored in relationship to other general practices and process areas. |
| Level 4:<br>Managed | At this point performance metrics are collected, analyzed and acted upon. The metrics are used to predict performance and provide better understanding of the processes and capabilities. |
| Level 5:<br>Optimizing | The processes are mature. Targets have been set for effectiveness and efficiency based on business and technical goals. There are ongoing refinements and improvements based on the understanding of the impact the changes bring to these processes. |

*EA Maturity Levels*

The following diagram depicts the EA Maturity assessment approach:

### Step 1: Finalize Framework
- Define assessment Parameters
- Define EA maturity levels

### Step 2: Prepare Questionnaire Survey for:
- Application Owners
- Directors
- CIO
- Operations

### Step 3: Collection and Analysis
- Collect responses from stakeholders
- Feed responses into the EA assessment tool
- Analyze and evaluate results

### Step 4: Maturity Assessment
- Assessment against each parameters
- Finalize the current and target maturity level

### Step 5: Present Assessment Report
- Finalize and present the report consisting of EA
- Current & target maturity levels, findings and observations, gaps and impact assessment.

The Maturity Score Card describes the maturity scores with respect to each of the architecture elements and their maturity level on the basis of the maturity assessment exercise which was conducted across the organization. The following diagram depicts the sample Maturity Score Card.

Maturity within the architecture framework will vary across the business architecture, business processes, technology architecture, as well as the architecture blueprint. This is an ever-evolving process that leads to an efficient, effective, responsive development and support organization.

### *Objective of EA Transformation*

The role of IT has shifted over the years. Instead of merely providing support for the business and its priorities, IT has evolved into an equal partner, actively participating in the decision-making process and developing initiatives together with the business. Making IT systems more cost efficient is not an easy task. It requires careful assessment, planning and phased implementation. Any changes to production IT systems can cause disruption, require additional expenses, and create temporary inconveniences. Radical changes often face resistance and difficulties in the organization. However, without fundamentally changing the way IT looks at its application portfolio and application lifecycle, it is impossible to increase agility and provide opportunities for innovation and future business growth. The top rationalization approach involves standardizing the application portfolio by reducing the number of custom built IT solutions and moving toward a more common set of applications, technologies, and infrastructure throughout the company.

## Important goals of company CIOs

- Create value for business
- Create better business alignment
- Improve flexibility of IT systems
- Increase quality of applications
- Innovate new application
- Increase productivity
- Improve efficiency through IT systems
- Cut Cost of IT
- Cut Overall cost for the business

## Application modernization can bring significant benefits like:

- Better aligned application landscape
- Reduced IT operating costs
- Improved agility of existing applications
- Tighter alignment with the business
- Better compliance with data retention regulations and easier access to archived records
- Improved processes going forward to prevent future problems
- Renewed focus on innovation

### *Challenges for EA Transformation*

Companies do not go overnight from streamlined, rationalized systems to a tangled landscape of redundant and outdated systems. It happens over long periods of time, sometimes following large events like corporate mergers, other times just through organic growth and development. There are several reasons why application landscapes have grown so complex.

Research has identified the following key reasons for IT application landscape complexity:

- Mergers and acquisitions result in many redundant systems with duplicate functionality.

- Custom legacy applications are becoming obsolete and are difficult to maintain, support, and integrate into the new, modern standardized IT infrastructure.
- Companies continue to support applications that no longer deliver full business value and do not support current business processes.
- Most organizations have data retention and archiving policy, but in reality the majority of companies are not willing to archive application data for fear of violating industry and government retention requirements.

When companies join together their IT systems, a number of applications are inevitably going to perform duplicate functions. Unfortunately, few companies have a clear strategy for archiving the data from obsolete applications and decommissioning redundant systems over time. A much more typical outcome of a merger or acquisition is to have multiple systems running in parallel for years, often lacking a significant user base, not properly integrated into the company's reporting and other IT systems, and causing a major strain on IT resources.

The other common cause for application complexity is custom applications. Traditionally, most companies chose to build their own custom systems to support their unique business processes and to gain fast competitive advantage. Surveys indicate that nearly half of all the applications in the IT portfolios of large corporations are custom-built.

Naturally, the number of custom-built systems varies depending on the company size; bigger companies with large IT teams traditionally develop more custom applications than their small and medium counterparts. But as companies grow, develop new product offerings, merge and acquire new business units, they begin to lose control of the rapidly growing number of custom-built applications and databases. Fast advances in technology make it increasingly difficult to maintain outdated legacy systems.

Of course, some of these legacy systems are still supporting key business processes and cannot be easily decommissioned or replaced with more modern solutions. Most IT portfolios, however, contain dozens, if not hundreds, of outdated legacy applications that are no longer considered business critical, but continue to be maintained for governance, compliance, data retention and other reasons. Often companies lack clear guidelines for retiring obsolete applications and archiving their data. As a result, outdated systems continue to plague IT landscapes, diverting resources away from innovation and growth.

In addition, companies have a problem with data retention. IT systems generate great quantities of data, which can grow exponentially, up to 5% per month on a large system. Not only does this uncontrollable data growth increase storage requirements, it becomes increasingly difficult to manage, search and retrieve. Most companies keep their application data for compliance purposes but in reality IT organizations often lack clear guidelines for archiving and retaining data, and as a result, companies tend to keep their data far beyond any required retention period.

### *Summary*

Transformation changes the entire application landscape or large portions of landscape. Transformations due to mergers, acquisitions or overhaul to processes tend to bring a radical change to the entire business landscape and by association its entire IT.

*Merger:* In mergers or acquisitions, the disparate application landscapes have to grow and blend into a common landscape.

*Demerger:* When an enterprise spins off parts of its operation, the application landscape has to be modified accordingly, and non-essential parts have to be removed.

*Overhaul:* To stay competitive in the market place, enterprises overhaul the entire IT and processes landscape to progress to a future state.

Such transformations typically involve an organization's business processes, IT and the master data transformation. The process involves assessing the maturity along with IT Landscape assessment. The methodology discussed in the next chapter requires transforming from a landscape of today to a landscape of tomorrow. The transformation journey also involves gap analysis, recommendations, and a roadmap to migrate from current state EA to future state EA.

# 3. EA Transformation Methodology

To gain control of the application portfolio and reduce complexity, organizations need to develop a strategic roadmap for EA transformation. This is possible with a structured and methodical approach which will also ensure the organization's future prosperity. The road to application transformation begins with identifying and implementing four fundamental steps:

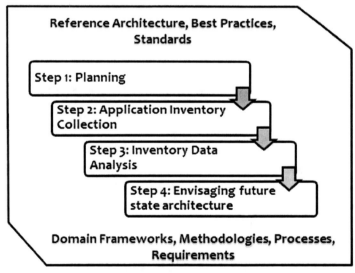

*EA Transformation Approach*

### Transformation Methodology

### Step 1: Planning

The key activity in the planning phase is gaining an understanding of the scope of the EA transformation initiative. This requires finalizing the governance structure, the team organization, project charter, roadmap, tools and the deliverables. This phase also requires the team to work on building assessment frameworks required for scanning and collecting inventory which is also a key step in any EA transformation project. This step also includes ramping up domain frameworks and reference architectures as applicable to the domain under consideration. This step also includes identifying the amount of customization required for the frameworks selected for the initiative.

EA Transformation Phases:
- Project Charter and Project Plan
- As-Is Architecture
- To-Be Architecture
- Gap/Impact Analysis
- IT Roadmap and Recommendations
- Knowledge Transfer

## Step 2: Application Inventory Collection

As part of the assessment phase a questionnaire is created to capture the current state, pain areas, gaps, issues and challenges in the current landscape.

This phase involves documenting the current state consisting of application architecture, technology architecture, business architecture and data architecture. These also consist of the interrelationships between applications and their dependencies.

## Step 3: Inventory Data Analysis

The most important step is to scan, analyze, and visualize your existing application portfolio, understand how it aligns with the business objective and goals and compare it with industry standards, best practices and reference architectures. This canvas gives the enterprise architect a strategic view to make decisions based on different solution scenarios.

There are many criteria – objective and subjective – that can be applied to identify which applications should be kept in their current state, which ones should be changed, and which are deemed obsolete and are candidates for retirement. These criteria are often referred to as filters and involve many different aspects of functional, structural, financial, and business relevance. It's not important to know how many users the application has; rather it is much more significant to understand the business criticality of each system and to what extent the application impacts revenue. It is essential to apply these filters to validate the initial understanding and create a complete and relevant picture of your applications' current states and future potential. These are generally done via the assessment frameworks as explained in the later sections. The following table describes various mechanisms for current state analysis of the application inventory.

| | Analysis | Description |
|---|---|---|
| 1 | Best Practice and Standards | Compare the landscape with industry standards and best practices |
| 2 | Cost Analysis | Understand the underlying costs of application as run/build, OPEX/CAPEX |
| 3 | Rationalization Analysis | Determine the ease of rationalization (how feasible it is to implement recommendations for expansion, restructuring, or consolidation of applications) |
| | | Find applications that are older with a smaller user base and minimal business functionality |
| | | Identify redundancies by company, country, business unit, plant, process, or function |

| Analysis | Description |
|---|---|
| 4 Comparative Analysis | Analyze different attributes and dimensions of an application (e.g. business value vs. cost; stability vs. criticality) |
| 5 Technology Alignment Analysis | Analyze the alignment of underlying application technology with preferred client technology |
| 6 Risk Analysis | Identify the risks associated with technology obsolescence, vendor support, skills availability, stability issues |

## Current State Analysis

This section describes the framework for rationalizing applications based on the strategy and value parameters.

*Strategy/Value Classification Methodology:*

One of the key methods involves building a strategy/value quadrant for the applications in the landscape. This application portfolio is based on the concept proposed by Harvard's Warren McFarlan. It maps the portfolio to a diagram consisting of four quadrants. This concise presentation of how IT contributes to present and future business success makes it a good tool to aid communication between business managers and IT professionals on plotting the future direction of the application landscapes.

Applications are classified according to their value contribution and strategy contribution. The value contribution indicates the extent to which a system supports business processes that create competitive advantage for the organization. The strategy contribution indicates how the system contributes to enacting corporate strategy; in other words, its part in the future business success of the enterprise. The portfolio's four quadrants are High Potential, Strategic, Operational and Support.

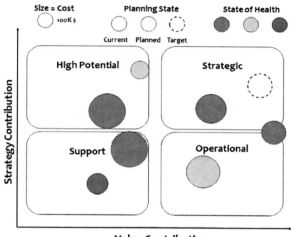

*Strategy Value Analysis*

The application qualities in each of the four quadrants are as described below:

*Strategic Applications*

Strategic controlling with a focus on efficiency and effectiveness:
- Provides clear competitive advantage accrued for the business through this application
- Application supports a specific business goal and/or a critical success factor

*High Potential*

Strategic Controlling with focus on cost cutting:
- Application leads to future benefit or value for the company

45

*Operations*

Operational Controlling with focus on efficiency and effectiveness:

- Application eliminates  an organization's disadvantage among its  competitors
- Application prevents a potential  business risk from becoming  a more serious  problem in the near future
- Application assists fulfillment of formal requirementsSupport
  Operational Controlling with focus on cost cutting:
- Application contributes to raising business productivity, or can  help achieve sustainable cost reduction

This framework can be utilized to facilitate decision making and building a target state.

## Step 4: Building the Target Architecture

The next step is to craft a future state architecture to increase efficiency of current applications, archive historical data, and safely retire obsolete IT systems. If the application is relevant for the business, it makes sense to continue investing in it. Many legacy applications still provide critical functionality, but are not as yet up-to-date and efficient. These applications need to be changed or modernized. They can be redeployed on modern servers, their codes can be updated to improve performance, or security can be enhanced to meet current standards. The outcome of this step is a gap analysis and a detailed go-forward plan to retire obsolete applications and archive outdated data. The next two sub sections describe the approach and strategies to transform the landscape and are very critical to a transformation journey.

46

The following paragraphs list a pragmatic approach for envisioning the future state application landscape. The combination of these techniques will facilitate building the landscape. Keep in mind as we review these steps that the best choice is always Simple and Robust as opposed to Complex and Unstable.

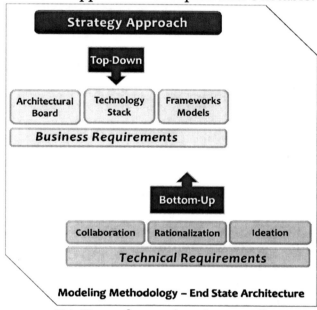

*EA Transformation Approach*

*Top-Down*

The Top-Down approach is ideal for meeting business expectations. The key input to this approach is IT strategy followed by business processes and functions (*aka business process maps) and application architectures. The Top-Down approach is primarily involved in defining a target environment aligned with industry benchmarks, standards and processes.

*Architecture Board*: The architecture board governs such areas as frameworks, standards, best practices and implementation choices.

*Technology Stacks:* Architecture board decides what technology platforms or product stacks are allowed for application development.

*Organization Models/Frameworks:* Organization modeling creates an overview of the organization structure depicting sub units and sub practices. Services and processes can be extracted based on such models.

*Bottom-Up*

In the Bottom-Up approach, the application landscape emerges from choices by business units, primarily involving identifying bottlenecks or weak links in the current system environment.

*Collaboration:* Requirements, components and interconnections between components are created as a collaborative effort among members from different departments and optionally, external vendors and partners.

*Rationalization:* Business should not create a large application estate. The strategy is rather to decommission applications, merge applications, or consolidate on selected technology platforms.

*Ideation:* Create ideas for new applications or extensions to the existing applications. The best ideas will be selected and unpopular applications will be retired.

Rationalization of applications is nothing but the removal of specific parts in the application ecosystem which will make the ecosystem leaner and more effective.

The top rationalization approach involves standardizing the application portfolio by reducing the number of custom built IT solutions and moving toward a more standardized set of applications, technologies, and infrastructure throughout the company. Consolidation, migration, replacement, renew, rewrite and simplification are popular rationalization strategies.

All of these strategies are closely related and should be implemented in conjunction with one another. For example, in order to standardize on a few selected applications and platforms, IT may choose to retire several duplicate systems, consolidate redundant functionality into one common solution, migrate old legacy applications onto modern platforms, and even potentially implement some of their applications in the Cloud to save on infrastructure costs.

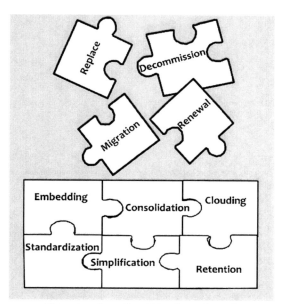

*Strategies for Modernization*

### EA Roadmap

The phased approach is the recommended approach as it reduces the risk and also ensures that the deployed solution is stable as compared to the big bang approach. The following diagram depicts an IT roadmap.

49

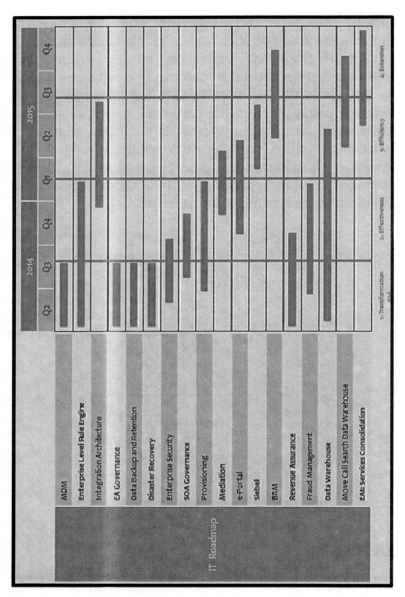

## Phased Approach: Advantages

- Improved efficiency and knowledge retention, as team rolls from one unit to another.

- Core solutions are optimized.
- Staggered requirement of business users.
- Best practices roll into the next phase.
- Change management is simpler.
- Master data would be defined at the first phase which would reduce effort in subsequent phases.
- Focus on one business unit at a time.
- Highly scalable design.
- Complete buy in of all the business units, right at the start; no 'surprises' later.

**Phased Approach: Disadvantages**

- Time to market is long.
- As focus is on one business unit at a time, the elapsed time for all the business units to go live will be long.
- Cost is incrementally high in Phased approaches.

*EA Risk Management*

There will always be risk with any architecture and business transformation efforts. It is important to identify, classify, and mitigate these risks before starting so that they can be tracked throughout the transformation effort. Mitigation is an ongoing effort and often the risk triggers may be outside the scope of the transformation planners (e.g., merger, acquisition), so planners must monitor the transformation context constantly. It is also important to note that the enterprise architect may identify the risks and mitigate certain ones, but it is within the governance framework that risks have to be first accepted and then managed.

There are two levels of risk that should be considered, namely:

*Initial Level of Risk:* Risk categorization prior to determining and implementing mitigating actions.

*Residual Level of Risk:* Risk categorization after implementation of mitigating actions (if any).

The process for risk management consists of the following activities:

- Risk classification
- Risk identification
- Initial risk assessment
- Risk mitigation and residual risk assessment
- Risk monitoring

## Enterprise Architecture Principles

Enterprise architectures will evolve over time and you cannot know everything you need to know up front in order to fully architect your system. Create your architecture with this evolution in mind so that it will be able to adapt to requirements that are not fully known at the start of the architecture process. Architecture principles should guide all technology decisions and support the strategic direction of the business.

| Architecture guiding principles are... | Guiding principles help organizations... |
|---|---|
| • Derived from the organization's core values<br>• Collection of statements used to assist in decision making<br>• They are not hard-and-fast rules<br>• Timeless in nature and change infrequently | • Establish criteria for new systems being introduced into the technical environment<br>• Steer technology planning and investment activities<br>• Inform decision-making – they are used as a guideline, but it is understood there are exceptions |

> Technology decision making is influenced by many things, but *ultimately decisions should support the business goals and objectives*

## EA Principles

The architecture principles can be categorized in various domains as depicted in the above diagram. Different principles, guidelines and standards will be applicable in the following key areas:

- *Enterprise Architecture:* Principles which apply across the application landscape to meet the business requirements.
- *Data:* Principles related to data ownership, access, management, quality, etc.
- *Security Management:* Principles covering authorization, authentication, privacy, etc.
- *Business Principles:* Principles for business architecture, processes, etc.
- *Application Principles:* Principles for application architecture, functional capabilities, application integration etc.
- *Integration:* Principles describing data and application interfaces, data transformation, data routing, etc.
- *Infrastructure:* Principles concerning hardware, networks, etc.

### *Summary*

Strategic use of IT will require a mindset change, away from a simplistic project-based culture where IT investment decisions were made based on a subjective value analysis, and where IT was responsible for building individual solutions and then getting them to work together. Enterprise architecture transformation focuses on converting, in multiple stages, a legacy, complex, spaghetti landscape to a full-fledged transformed digitized platform.

Transforming IT ultimately means managing IT to enable business agility, growth and cost rationalization. This transformation naturally leads to a step change in business performance resulting from development and increasing use of the digitized platform.

Creating a context for innovation and agility becomes essential for success in a Digital Economy. This will be achieved either via Business Process Exploitation (improving, extending or reusing existing capabilities) or Greenfield Exploration (investigating opportunities outside of existing capabilities) at enterprise or business unit levels. IT-Business Alignment will be further explored in the next chapter.

In the future, the role of the CIO is likely to expand to include generating revenue streams, at the same time cutting business costs, enabling globalization and business agility, and managing non-IT assets while still being held accountable for IT services.

# 4. Business & IT Alignment

Organizational models continue to evolve and management techniques continue to change, but IT business alignment and its close relative, process-technology alignment, remain as top objectives for most CIO's. Easier said than done, to be sure, and it's becoming increasingly difficult to do so. According to Gartner, "How technology will support growth and results is a fundamental question for the future. It is no longer sufficient to tend the IT garden and declare success. Digital technologies provide a platform to achieve results, but only if CIOs adopt new roles and behaviors to hunt for digital value. CIOs require a new agenda for digital business and beyond — an agenda that secures IT's future strategic role, funding and skills."

### *Defining IT-Business Alignment*

IT-Business Alignment is the dynamic state of a business when it effectively uses Information Technology to achieve overall business objectives. IT-Business Alignment involves the correlation between the business objectives and the IT requirements of an organization. Maintained over time, IT-Business Alignment is crucial to the success of a business, with flexible business plans and IT architectures acting as key components of alignment effort. IT-Business Alignment can also be seen as the capacity to demonstrate a positive relationship between IT and the customers of IT within the business groups that often struggle to unite because of differences in goals, culture, and incentives.

### *Problems with Misalignment*

Aligning IT with business strategy has been an ongoing topic of discussion among IT executives for many years. Although the issue has been recognized as an ongoing concern within organizations for decades, very little has been done to foster the alignment. Alignment entails more than the executive level communication of business strategy to IT; IT-Business Alignment requires action from both IT and the business executives to ensure that IT provides the services that directly contribute to business outcomes.

Nonetheless, a disconnect often exists between IT and other business units because of differences in cultural and structural barriers, as well as differing departmental objectives and goals. It is not unusual for an organization to experience a blame culture between business units and IT due to misperceptions. Additionally, the consequences of misalignment reach beyond an organization's corporate culture. Organizations that fail to align IT and business strategy face increasing financial costs. When IT within a business is not perceived as an enabler of business strategy, IT is not viewed as the provider of choice and ultimately risks being outsourced to a third party vendor. Alternately, some applications could be outsourced that are not compatible with existing IT systems or programs, compounding the cultural and structural disconnects.

### *Current Challenges with T-Business Alignment*

Often IT strategic goals and objectives are not in direct support of the business' goals and objectives. Not only does IT not speak the language of the business, but there is no meeting of the minds between what the business wants and what IT delivers. Most organizations have metrics that are technology focused, which have no meaning to the business units. For example, IT is satisfied when the printer is online; the end-user is dissatisfied when the printer will print everything but Adobe PDFs. IT often focuses on measuring availability of components such as servers, networks and applications and not the end-to-end delivery of business processes.

Ultimately, when IT acts as a separate, stand-alone business, the rest of the enterprise will treat it as a vendor and not as a partner. An organization's lack of IT-Business Alignment is not solely due to IT, as both IT and the business are stakeholders in fostering alignment. Business units have an equal responsibility for bringing about alignment. However, many IT decisions are often driven by business executives who may have a limited understanding of IT.

### *Starting With Strategy*

To align IT with the business, it is recommended to begin with the development of an IT strategy that will articulate the department's objectives, define how the department will meet those objectives and prescribe how the department will know it has met those objectives. A well-defined and managed IT strategy ensures that the resources and capabilities of the organization are aligned to desired business outcomes by matching IT investments with the organization's intended development and growth plan.

An effective IT strategy also ensures that IT has the appropriate set of services in its Service Portfolio, its services have a clear purpose, and everyone in the service provider organization knows his or her role in achieving that purpose. Strategy Management for IT services further encourages appropriate levels of investment that will result in cost savings, since investments and expenditures are matched to the achievement of validated business objectives rather than un-substantiated demands. Effective IT strategy can also result in increased levels of investment for key projects or service improvements. Shifting investment priorities can also happen when an IT strategy is effectively aligned with the business. The service provider will be able to defocus attention from one service and refocus on another, ensuring that efforts and budgets are spent on the areas with the highest level of business impact.

### *Way Forward*

With the increasing reliance on Information Technology and the necessity of IT services, IT-Business Alignment is now a necessary mindset of successful companies. For IT-Business Alignment to succeed in any size organization it should be viewed as not only a strategy and a set of best practices but as a company mandate that furthers a partnership with IT and Business. The alignment of IT and business strategy is a difficult challenge for many organizations, especially considering the immediate performance that is often expected of professionals. It is without question that IT-Business Alignment has been utilized by organizations to create and improve efficiencies, reduce costs, and ultimately create value to the business. When taking on the challenge of alignment, organizations should remember that IT-Business Alignment needs to be re-evaluated and reviewed at least annually and especially during modifications in corporate direction. For alignment to work, an organization's culture must embrace IT as an enabler and integral part of the long-term success of the organization.

### *Methodology for IT and Business Alignment*

The goal of *perfect* alignment is not achievable because of the dynamic nature of business. Every organization operates in an ecosystem and is affected by the forces at play in it. Economy, industry, competitors etc. are all players in this ecosystem that are continuously evolving. Similarly, knowledge and tools are also continuously changing. To remain competitive and maintain differentiation every organization must adapt in response to the actions and activities of others in its ecosystem. Organizations that do not adapt lose their competitive edge over time and disappear. The following steps should be adopted while going through the EA transformation journey.

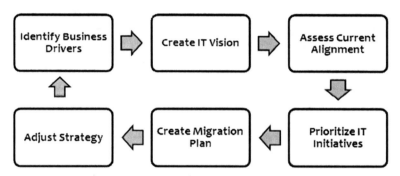

*Business & IT Alignment Approach*

## Step 1: Identify Business Drivers

In this step, we identify the business needs of the organization, i.e., the business needs that require IT enablement. E.g., is the company launching a new product that requires a new fulfillment system, or is the company acquiring another company that requires rationalizing the systems?

## Step 2: Create IT Vision

This step identifies the IT Capability – strategy, process, infrastructure and organization – required to meet business priorities. This vision lays the guidelines or policies that drive the creation of the IT Capability. It is very important to articulate these underlying attitudes and beliefs into a vision before attempting to answer the IT Capability question.

**Step 3: Assess Current Alignment**

This step answers the question: How does the current IT Capability compare to the envisioned IT Capability? There are three dimensions of alignment (investment, asset and organization). By answering this question for all three, this step assesses the alignment along these dimensions.

Comparing the desired or "to-be" IT Capability with the current or "as is" IT Capability, one can identify gaps that are causing misalignment. Again, this comparison is made along the three dimensions (investment, asset and organization) to precisely identify the root cause of misalignment. Once we have the root causes, we can identify the potential fixes. One "fix" can potentially address multiple gaps. This step provides the necessary inputs to understand the target capabilities that are required in the landscape and to start planning for the IT initiatives.

**Step 4: Prioritize IT Initiatives**

The previous step gives us a list of opportunities that require business and IT alignment. Some opportunities are easier than others. Some provide greater business value and have to be prioritized accordingly.

A prioritized list of "fixes" or IT Initiatives is the starting point for implementation planning. This is a critical step to ensure success. Often, organizations forget to plan for implementation and pay the price in terms of over-budget or delayed or failed projects. This step takes the list of initiatives and creates a roadmap for IT. This roadmap is a result of careful planning that is driven by multiple factors including risk, cost and time.

**Step 5: Create Migration Plan**

This step creates a migration plan for the IT roadmap – steps, deliverables, responsibility, timing etc. It needs to address these key elements. The plan should also be modified as we learn new things after implementation begins.

**Step 6: Adjust IT Strategy**

This is the key step to ensure connection between the changing business needs while we are implementing IT solutions. It is essential that we keep track of the changing business world, both internal and external, and make sure that our solutions are in line. If not, the senior leadership has the responsibility to ensure that we do not continue those initiatives.

*Summary*

Alignment between IT and the business has become increasingly critical as we pass through the client-server era, where enterprise technology was defined by IT, and into an era defined by the business with digital technology. Market leaders will be those for whom process and technology have unified to deliver enterprise-wide benefits.

# 5. Documenting Enterprise Architecture

Documenting the architecture is the crowning step to crafting it. Even a perfect architecture is useless if no one understands it or if key stakeholders misunderstand it. If you go to the trouble of creating a strong architecture, you must describe it in sufficient detail, without ambiguity, and organize in such a way that others can quickly find needed information. Otherwise, your effort will have been wasted because the architecture will be unusable. Architecture documentation is both prescriptive and descriptive. That is, for some audiences it prescribes what should be true by placing constraints on decisions to be made. For other audiences, it describes what is true by recounting decisions already made about a system's design.

## Introduction

Architecture is an artifact for early analysis to make sure that a given design approach will yield an acceptable system. Moreover, architecture holds the key to post-deployment system understanding, maintenance, and mining efforts. In short, architecture is the conceptual glue that holds every phase of a project together for all of its many stakeholders. The architecture serves as the blueprint for both the system and the project developing it. It defines the work assignments that must be carried out by design and implementation teams and it is the primary carrier of system qualities such as performance, modifiability, and security, none of which can be achieved without a unifying architectural vision. The architecture for a system depends on the requirements levied on it; so too does the documentation for architecture depend on the requirements levied on it; that is how we expect it will be used. Documentation is decidedly not a case of one size fits all. It should be sufficiently abstract to be quickly understood by new employees but sufficiently detailed to serve as a blueprint for analysis. The architectural documentation for, say, security analysis may well be different from the architectural documentation we would hand to an implementer. And both of these will be different from what we put in a new hire's familiarization reading list.

### *Stakeholders and Communication Needs Served by Architecture*

All of this tells us that different stakeholders for the documentation have different needs, different kinds of information, and different levels of information and different treatments of information. We should not expect to produce one architectural document and have every consumer read it in the same way. Rather, we should produce documentation that helps a stakeholder quickly find the information that he or she is interested in, with a minimum of information that is irrelevant standing in the way. This might mean producing different documents for different stakeholders. More likely, it means producing a single documentation suite with a roadmap that will help different stakeholders navigate through it. One of the most fundamental rules for technical documentation in general, and software architecture documentation in particular, is to write from the point of view of the reader.

Perhaps one of the most avid consumers of architectural documentation is none other than the architect, at some point in the project's future; someone guaranteed to have an enormous stake in it. New architects are interested in learning how their predecessors tackled the difficult issues of the system and why particular decisions were made.

### *Architectural Views*

The most important concept associated with software architecture documentation is the *view*. A view is a representation of a coherent set of architectural elements, as written by and read by system stakeholders. A structure is the set of elements itself, as they exist in software or hardware.

Software architecture is a complex entity that cannot be described in a simple one-dimensional fashion. The analogy with building architecture, if not taken too far, proves illuminating. There is no single rendition of a building architecture, but many: the room layouts, the elevation drawings, the electrical diagrams, the plumbing diagrams, the ventilation diagrams, the traffic patterns, the sunlight and passive solar views, the security system plans, and many others.

The concept of a view, which you can think of as capturing a structure, provides us with the basic principle for documenting software architecture. Documenting architecture is a matter of documenting the relevant views and then adding documentation that applies to more than one view. This principle is useful because it breaks the problem of architecture documentation into more tractable parts.

### Choosing an Architectural View

The many purposes that architecture can serve — as a mission statement for implementers, as the starting point for system understanding and asset recovery, as the blueprint for project planning, and so forth — are each represented by a stakeholder wanting and expecting to use the documentation to serve that purpose. Similarly, the quality attributes of most concern

64

to you and the other stakeholders in the system's development will affect the choice of what views to document. For instance, a layered view will tell you about your system's portability. A deployment view will let you reason about your system's performance and reliability. These quality attributes are covered in the documentation by analysts who need to examine the architecture to make sure the quality attributes are provided.

In short, different views support different goals and uses. This is fundamentally why we do not advocate a particular view or a collection of views. The views you should document depend on the uses you expect to make of the documentation. Different views will highlight different system elements and/or relationships.

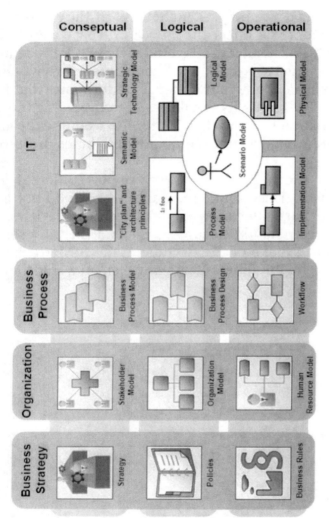

*Enterprise Architecture Views*

## *Identifying Business Capabilities in the Value Chain*

This section and the next will outline the process of creating business capabilities and building the business capabilities map. These are the initial steps to determine the capabilities that an enterprise needs and that are subsequently supported by the IT systems.

Michael Porter describes that value is created through the chain of activities for a company that operates in a specific industry. For gaining the competitive advantage, Porter suggested that going through the chain of activities will add more value to the products and services than the sum of added cost of these activities. And thus, a company will gain marginal value for a given product or service.

The value chain framework can be used as a powerful analysis tool for strategic planning and to build the organizational model, ensuring an effective leadership model. The value chain concept can be applied to an individual business unit and can be extended to the whole supply chain and distribution networks. To create a successful product for an organization it is important to add value in each activity that the product goes through during the life cycle. For that it needs all, or a combination of value chain activities and a proper synchronization among all the related activities. A proper value chain requires that it contains all the required functional departments to perform the activities and a proper communication approach is required to synchronize the activities of these functional units efficiently.

**Problem**

The challenge is how to map Porter's Value Chain activities into functional business activities. To solve this problem, first we have to classify the value chain activities into functional activities.

*Classification of Porter's Value Chain activities.* Porter classified the generic value added activities into two classes which are presented in the figure below.

67

These activities are: *primary activities* which are classified as product and market related activities and *support activities* that are related to infrastructure, technology, procurement, and human resource management.

Primary activities can be classified into product related and market related activities that are described below:

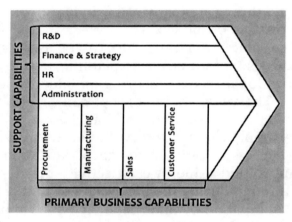

*Product related activities.* The activities that the organization performs to add value to the products and services are classified as inbound logistics, operations, or services.

- *Inbound logistics:* For the production and development activities, organizations need inputs as goods that are received from suppliers. Inbound logistics refer to all the activities related to receiving goods from suppliers, decisions about the transportation scheduling, storing the goods as inventory, managing the inventory, and making the inputs ready to use for the production of end products.

- *Operations:* These include the production process, development activities, testing, packaging, mainte-

68

nance, and all other activities that transform the inputs into finished product.

- *Services:* Organizations offer services after the products and/or services have been sold. These service activities enhance the product's value in the form of after sales guarantees, warranties, spare parts management, repair services, installation, updating, trainings, etc.

**Market Related Activities.** The activities that the organization performs to transfer the finished products or services to customers are market related activities and in a bird's-eye view these activities are classified as either outbound logistics or marketing and sales.

- *Outbound Logistics:* The finished products are developed using the product related activities. Now activities are required to transfer the finished products to the customers via warehousing, order fulfilment, transportation, and distribution management.
- *Marketing and Sales:* These activities include the advertising, channel selection, product promotion, selling, product pricing, retail management, etc. The activities are performed to make sure that the products are transferred to the targeted customer groups. Marketing mix can be an instrument to take the competitive advantage to the target customers.

**Support activities.** These are the activities that organization performs to assist the primary activities to gain the competitive advantage more broadly are classified as procurement, technology management, human resource management, or infrastructure activities.

- *Procurement:* This is the purchasing activity of the inputs to transform raw materials into finished

69

products or services. Procurement adds value by the acquisition of appropriate goods or services at the best price, at the right time, and in the desired place with the desired quality and quantity.

- *Technology Management:* This is very important in today's technology-driven environment. Technology can be used in production to reduce cost, to develop new products, increase customer service, build up cost effective processes. It supports the value chain activities such as research and development, process automation, process design, etc.

- *Human Resource Management:* The key roles of HR are to support the attainment of the overall strategic business plan and the objectives. As a strategic business partner HR designs the work positions by hiring, recognition, reward, appraisal systems, career planning, and employee development. HR acts as an advocate for the employees to motivate them and create a happy working environment. For the organizational change situation, HR executes the strategic needs of the organization with minimum employee dissatisfaction and resistance to change.

- *Infrastructure:* This includes the planning management, legal framework, financing, accounting, public affairs, quality management, general management, etc. These are required to perform the value added activities efficiently to drive the organization forward to meet the strategic plan and the objectives.

## Solution: Mapping Porter's Value Chain activities into business functionalities

The product related activities can be divided among functional units: production performs operational activities, partly inbound logistics, and services activities. Software production includes the activities as product development, testing, packaging, maintenance, installation, updating, training, etc. The sales function performs part of the services activities (e.g. guarantees, warranties). Inbound logistics activities can be shared between logistics department and the production function, as an inventory management activity. In SMEs, the logistics department can be merged with marketing and the sales unit. In brief, the function of production management is to manage the production activities to meet the strategic goals.

*Market related activities* can be classified as a function of marketing and sales. In many organizations marketing and sales are two independent departments that work in collaboration. But in SMEs both departments can be merged into one department to perform all the related activities. The decision process of marketing and sales depends on the revenue and cost element of all the marketing and sales activities.

*Technology Management activities* can be presented as the research and development (R&D) function which increases the stock of knowledge for the organization. Infrastructure related activities can be divided into key business functions of general management, finance and accounting, and quality management. For SMEs, procurement activities may belong to the marketing and sales department in collaboration with production operations, for scaling the need of quality and quantity.

*Infrastructure related activities* can be divided into key business functions of general management, finance and accounting, quality management and general management. Depending on the size of the organization, procurement activities may belong to the marketing and sales department in collaboration with production operations for scaling the need of quality and quantity.

## Stepwise Approach

- *Step-1:* Depending on the business model, we have to find the organizational value chain activities.
- *Step-2:* The defined value chain activities have to be assigned to proper value added business functions.
- *Step-3:* Define a proper organizational structure such that each business unit can generate the effective maximum value by performing all necessary value added activities.
- *Step-4:* Define proper synchronization mechanisms for the efficient synchronization of business functional activities to achieve common business goals.
- *Step-5:* Define effective communication mechanisms among the business functional units.

### *Business Capability Modeling*

The simplest business model involves creating a product and selling it directly to customers. Other models involve selling wholesale to retailers, selling through distributors, licensing products to other companies, selling online, selling through auctions, and countless other alternatives. No one-size-fits-all solution exists. In fact, most companies use some combination of business models to arrive at a unique model.

Step one in building a successful business is to learn what products or technologies your customers really need and are willing to buy. This is an iterative process. The vast majority of technology startups fail because too few customers buy or use their products.

72

So don't underestimate the importance of validating and testing your ideas.

Developing the right product is hard. But what is harder is building a good business model. Fortunately, there's nothing magical about a business model. It's simply the nuts and bolts of how a business plans to generate revenue and profits. It details your long-term strategy and day-to-day operations.

## Constructing Business Capabilities

Business capabilities have quickly become the core element of most business architecture models. Their appeal is largely driven by three factors. First, business leaders at all levels find capabilities an appealing and useful way to think about growing their organization's impact. Second, capabilities are versatile, easily applied to high level strategic activities such as scenario planning or outsourcing investigations as well as lower level operational analysis. And third, capabilities can be linked to other elements in the planning process such as people, process, technology, and information.

However, capabilities remain poorly understood and often confused with processes, functions, or services. Let's look at capabilities from these perspectives:

*Capability Model Structure.* A capability model describes the complete set of capabilities an organization requires to execute its business model or fulfill its mission. It might also be referred to as a capability map or a capability canvas. Capability models are multilevel but the numbers of levels vary greatly from organization to organization depending on how the model is applied. Almost all have at least two levels with very few having more than five. Currently there is no accepted standard for capability structure.

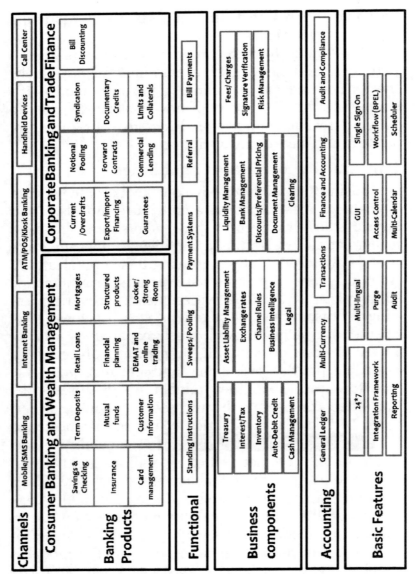

*Business Capability Map*

- *First level capabilities organize the model:* The highest level of a capability model is generally referred to as level one. Early modelers often referred to this level as level zero but that terminology has fallen out of favor as capability models have become more business centric. The purpose of level one is to provide a logical way to organize the lower levels and create a focused starting point to flesh out the rest of the model. Some organizations use level one purely as a categorization mechanism where the categories do not represent capabilities themselves but are simply labels. The value of this approach is that the top level structure can change to fit the audience, reorganizing lower level capabilities to fit the context. Common approaches to creating the top level structure utilize the organization's value chain, value streams, major functions, or business segments. Most models have between five and ten categories or capabilities at this level. To identify top level capabilities is to define them as the major elements of the organization's value chain. Business leaders resonate with this view and can quickly identify and come to consensus on the top level elements. In this approach, the level one capabilities are true capabilities that can be described with the same attributes as lower level capabilities.
- *Second level capabilities create the core model:* Level two is considered the core capability model. Many organizations do not go any deeper. A well-constructed level two model will provide the details necessary to facilitate strategic discussions and resource analysis. Capabilities at this level will completely describe the entire organization being modeled, but not necessarily at a consistent level of de-

tail. For example a high-tech consumer products company might have ten or more capabilities related to innovation but only have one for HR or IT. This imbalance simply reflects management's viewpoint on the important contributors to their business model. The number of level two capabilities varies greatly depending on the complexity of the organization being modeled and the intended usage. Most models have between 40 and 100 capabilities. With fewer than 20, it becomes difficult to perform any meaningful resource analysis or improvement design. With more than 100, the model becomes too complex to facilitate strategic discussions and will be relegated to operational analysis activities.

- *Third level capabilities provide more insight to level two capabilities:* Level three capabilities can be thought of as sub-capabilities of their parent, level two. Their fundamental role is to provide further detail to level two capabilities by describing more discrete components. Modeling to level three creates better understanding of the level two capabilities used in strategic planning and ensures the correct capabilities are represented in level two (during the level three modeling, important level three capabilities are promoted to level two and less important level two capabilities are demoted to level three).

- *Lower level capabilities link to operational activities:* Capability views below level three are primarily used by solution designers and implementers to connect the model to processes and technologies. These levels are developed much less often than higher levels and are typically seen in organizations that have either a mature management-by-

76

capability approach or utilize capability modeling largely from an operational viewpoint.

- In many models, levels four and below represent process steps or activities. While this might not strictly adhere to the principles of capability modeling, it can be a very useful way to connect the strategic views created at levels one and two to the operational work necessary to support them.

## Business Capabilities Maps

A business capability map is a model of the firm associating the business capabilities, processes, and functions required for business success with the IT resource that enables them.

*Business Capability Map:* Business capabilities represent an organization's business, independent of organization structure, processes, or people. The Capability Model is the Enterprise's anchor model.

*Business Architecture:* The business architecture defines the overall structure of solutions that implement and embody a given business capability. At the lowest level they are represented as business processes.

*Logical/Application Architecture:* The logical architecture shows the systems components need to enable the capability. The best practice is to create shared or reusable components.

*Physical Architecture:* The technology or physical architecture provides the deployment view of the landscape depicting servers, storage, network elements and security components.

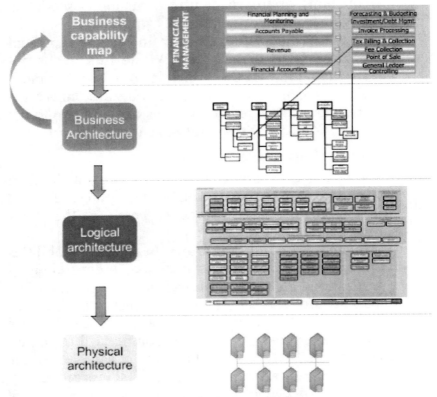

*Business Capability Modeling*

## *Typical Contents of EA Documents*

An enterprise architecture document describes the salient ideas in the architecture, including the decisions of architectural analysis. Practically, it is a learning aid for all stakeholders who need to understand the essential ideas of the system.

When someone joins the EA team, it's useful if the project coach can say, "Welcome to the NextGen project. Please go to the project website and read the EA document in order to get an overview." Therefore, it should be written with this audience and goal in mind, e.g. "What do I need to say that will quickly help someone understand the major ideas?"

An architectural view is a tool of communication, education, or thought; it is expressed in the form of text and diagrams.

In the EA document, the architect will create a section called the Logical View, insert diagrams, and add some written description on what each package and/or component and layer is for, and the motivation behind the logical design.

Architectural views may be created:

- After the system is built, as a summary and as a learning aid for future developers
- At the end of certain iteration milestones (such as the end of elaboration) to serve as a learning aid for the current development team, and new members
- Speculatively, during early iterations, as an aid in creative design work, recognizing that the original view will change as design and implementation proceeds

## EA Documents – Capturing the Details

*Introduction:* Consists of document objective, scope and audience, stakeholder and communication protocol and/or charter.

*Architectural Representation:* Summary of how the architecture will be described in this document, such as by using technical memos and the architectural views. This is useful for someone unfamiliar with the idea of technical memos or views. Note that not all views are necessary.

*Architectural Factors:* Reference to the Supplementary Specification to view the Factor Table.

*Architectural Decisions:* The set of technical memos that summarize the decisions.

*Architectural Principles:* The set of architectural principles that should be followed as part of the EA process.

*Approach Methodology:* Approach and Methodology that is followed during the complete EA process.

*Company Vision and Objective:* Company Vision and Objective and how that will be realized by the EA.

*Application View:* Package diagrams, and class diagrams of major elements. Commentary on the large scale structure and functionality of major components.

*Technology View:* Deployment diagrams showing the nodes and allocation of processes and components. Commentary on the networking.

*Business View:* Class and interaction diagrams illustrating the processes and threads of the system. Group this by threads and processes that interact. Comment on how the inter- process communication works.

*Use-Case View:* Brief summary of the most architecturally significant use cases. Interaction diagrams for some architecturally significant use case realizations, or scenarios, with commentary on the diagrams explaining how they illustrate the major architectural elements.

*Reference Architect and Domain Frameworks:* The reference architecture and domain frameworks as applicable to the domain e.g. eTOM, SID, ITITL etc.

*Architecture Governance:* guidance on how the future and current architecture would be governed as part of the EA process.

## *Summary*

Documenting architecture is the crowning step in creating a useful Enterprise Architecture, freeing the architect from having to answer hundreds of questions about it and serving to capture it for current and future stakeholders.

Treat the task of documenting architecture as documenting the set of relevant views and then supplementing that with cross-view information. Use the stakeholders to help choose the relevant views.

This chapter presented a prescriptive organization for documenting software architectures. You may ask why we have not strictly adhered to it in the architectural case studies in this book. A fundamental principle of technical documentation of any kind – and software architecture documentation in particular – is to write so that the material is of the most use for the anticipated readers. Here, the reader wants an overview of the system, its motivations, and how it meets its quality goals.

# 6. EA Governance

Architecture Governance is the practice and orientation by which enterprise architectures and other architectures are monitored, managed and controlled. Architecture Governance is required to ensure the principles of Enterprise Architecture are applied to both systems architecture and design of the underlying information systems. It also ensures organizations meet business and IT objectives and standards. Architecture Governance enables effective alignment of business and information technology, manages risk by reducing probability of failures in transformation projects, and incorporates elements of cost effectiveness and value.

### Introduction
Architecture Governance includes the following:

- Implementing a system of controls over the creation and monitoring of all architectural components and activities, to ensure the effective introduction, implementation, and evolution of architectures within the organization
- Implementing a system to ensure compliance with internal and external standards and regulatory obligations
- Establishing processes that support effective management of the processes within agreed parameters
- Developing practices that ensure accountability to a clearly identified stakeholder community, both inside and outside the organization

Architecture Governance typically operates within a hierarchy of governance structures which, particularly in the larger enterprise, can include the following as distinct domains with their own disciplines and processes:

- Corporate Governance
- Technology Governance
- IT Governance
- Architecture Governance

Each of these domains of governance may exist at multiple geographic levels – global, regional, and local – within the overall enterprise.

### *Architecture Governance Framework*

EA drives transformation and acts as a catalyst for change. While several organizations adopt EA for transformation, each organization's experience varies based on its inherent culture, EA maturity and IT landscape. Architecture Governance (AG) is an integral part of IT Governance and imperative for both EA effectiveness and for an organization to succeed in transformation initiatives.

### Conceptual Structure

Architecture Governance is an approach, a series of processes, a cultural orientation, and a set of owned responsibilities that ensure the integrity and effectiveness of the organization's architectures. It is well accepted that synergies between people, process and technology is the key to success. AG framework can be reused for other transformation programs albeit in the context of specific program needs.

| Organization | Processes | Tools |
|---|---|---|
| • Steering Committee | • Approach and Plan | • Architecture Modelling Tools |
| • Architecture Board | • Configuration & Release Management | • Collaboration Tools |
| • Architecture Team | • Compliance | • Architecture Repository |
| • Architecture Stakeholders | • Risk Management | • Project Management Tools |
| • Architecture Sub Groups & Forums | • Communication | |
| | • Change Control | |

83

*Organization:* includes the people and structures that collaborate to deliver the transformation program objectives and comprises the following core elements:

- The program steering committee that provides executive sponsorship
- The program architectural board that oversees the development of the architecture and manages and controls change
- The program architecture team comprising business and IT components and is responsible for addressing integration aspects
- The architecture program/project management team that brings discipline into the architecture work
- The project architects and business analysts that is responsible for addressing project architectural aspects
- The architecture stakeholder groups that provide inputs required to perform architecture activities, receive outputs arising out of performed architecture activities and receive information about architecture activities and perform related activities
- The program stakeholder groups and forums that involve architecture team participation
- The architecture forums that build the collaborative mechanisms for the stakeholders and ensure alignment
- The architecture audit teams that ensure adherence to the architecture framework

*Processes:* Provide the delivery mechanisms for the architecture team and comprise the following core elements:

- An approach to develop the program architecture

- The architecture plan which translates the approach into an actionable work breakdown structure
- The change control process that refines the architecture based on various inputs
- The review processes to ensure the quality and acceptance of the architecture outputs
- The compliance process that enforces adherence to the architecture
- The configuration and release management processes that control the issue of architecture documents for consumption by intended audience
- The risk management process that lays out the architectural risks and mitigation strategies
- The reporting process to track and report the work being delivered
- The communication processes to align the stakeholders and enable decision making
- The program/project management processes that ensure program alignment while managing architecture work

*Tools:* enable the organization and processes to deliver with reduced effort and comprise of the following core elements:

- Comprehensive modelling tools that allow creation of holistic EA artefacts
- Collaboration tools that support collaboration
- Architecture repository that provides a structure for cataloguing and viewing various architecture components
- Project management tools to plan and manage EA tasks
- Supporting tools such as survey tools to capture Voice of Customer blogs to foster discussions, etc.

85

## Organizational Structure

The key factors influencing the implementation of an AG framework are program needs, the organization's culture, the program/project management maturity, the architecture function maturity, the need for the speedy assembly of people from various vendors in addition to customer staff, the mindset of the architects versus project managers, and reusability of current processes and tools.

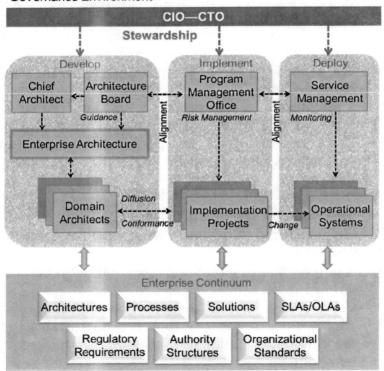

*EA Governance Organization*

### Architecture Board

An important element in any Architecture Governance strategy is establishment of a cross-organizational

86

Architecture Board to oversee the implementation of the governance strategy. This body should be representative of all the key stakeholders in the architecture, and will typically comprise a group of executives responsible for the review and maintenance of the overall architecture. The costs of establishing and operating an Architecture Board are more than offset by the savings that accrue as a result of preventing one-off solutions and unconstrained developments across the enterprise, which invariably lead to:

- High costs of development
- High costs of operation and support
- Numerous run-time environments
- Numerous implementation languages
- Numerous interfaces and protocols
- Lower quality
- Higher risk
- Difficulty in replicating and reusing solutions

The Architecture Board is made responsible and accountable for achieving some or all of the following goals:

- Consistency between sub-architectures
- Identifying re-usable components
- Flexibility of enterprise architecture; to meet business needs and utilize new technologies
- Enforcement of Architecture Compliance
- Improving the maturity level of architecture discipline within the organization
- Ensuring that the discipline of architecture based development is adopted
- Providing the basis for all decision making with regard to changes to the architectures
- Supporting a visible escalation capability for out of bounds decisions

The Architecture Board is also responsible for operational items such as the monitoring and control of Architecture Contracts, and for governance items such as producing usable governance materials.

### *Benefits of Architecture Governance*

Architecture Governance is beneficial because it:

- Links IT processes, resources, and information to organizational strategies and objectives
- Integrates and institutionalizes IT best practices
- Aligns with industry frameworks such as COBIT (planning and organizing, acquiring and implementing, delivering and supporting, and monitoring IT performance)
- Enables the organization to take full advantage of its information, infrastructure, and hardware/software assets
- Protects the underlying digital assets of the organization
- Supports regulatory and best practice requirements such as auditability, security, responsibility, and accountability
- Promotes visible risk management

### *Summary*

Architecture Governance is the practice and orientation by which enterprise architectures and other architectures are managed and controlled at an enterprise-wide level. It includes the following:

- Implementing a system of controls over the creation and monitoring of all architecture components and activities, to ensure the effective introduction, implementation, and evolution of architectures within the organization

88

- Implementing a system to ensure compliance with internal and external standards and regulatory obligations
- Establishing processes that support effective management of the above processes within agreed parameters
- Developing practices that ensure accountability to a clearly identified stakeholder community, both inside and outside the organization

The Architecture Board oversees the implementation of the governance strategy. Its members are representatives of all the key stakeholders in the architecture, typically a group of executives responsible for the review and maintenance of the overall architecture.

Architecture Contracts are joint agreements between development partners and sponsors on the deliverables, quality, and fitness-for-purpose of an architecture. Successful implementation of these agreements will be delivered through effective Architecture Governance. Ensuring the compliance of individual projects within the enterprise architecture is an essential aspect of Architecture Governance.

# 7. Architecture Assurance

The aim of Architecture Assurance is to provide collaborative architecture processes for assuring complete implementation of the technical solutions that are aligned with the business drivers of an enterprise in a timely environment. Effective sharing of the information across different Business Units (BU) or departments within an enterprise and interoperability across IT systems would ensure the alignment of IT with business. The Architecture Assurance Group (AAG) is involved in reviewing the Project Architecture during the design and development phases of an application/system to help ensure successful project implementation. This review also ensures that the proposed system fits into the existing enterprise environment as well as the future architecture vision. The goals of Architecture Assurance include some or all of the following:

- Identify inconsistencies in the architecture early, which reduces the cost and risk of changes required later in the life cycle
- Provide an overview of the compliance of architecture to mandated enterprise standards
- Identify where the standards may require modification
- Identify services that are currently application-specific but might be provided as part of the enterprise infrastructure
- Take advantage of advances in technology
- Communicate to management the status of the technical readiness of the project

- Identify and communicate significant architectural gaps to product and service providers
- Establish, own and manage Enterprise Architecture Content
- Provide architecture governance: guidelines and recommendations on business and IT architecture
- Ensure and enforce architecture compliance: review changes and deviations in business and IT architecture
- Resolve architectural ambiguities, issues and conflicts at the enterprise level
- Identify projects that have high architectural risk, and provide assistance to them early and often throughout the project
- Provide guidance to project managers and designers to direct architecture compliance
- Formally review projects to ensure compliance
- Leverage third-party assessments
- Leverage COTS's products

The main benefits of these reviews are:
- Project Success
- Architecture is reviewed by a group of experienced architects across the enterprise
- Assistance in leveraging the existing architecture promoting the reusability
- Architecture for plug and play
- Promote simplification and standardization
- Proactively identify risks to the project
- Provide enterprise-wide context to project team
- Maintains the integrity of the enterprise IT environment and expands the user community's access to Enter resources

- Identifies if the project presents risk to the IT environment (e.g., infrastructure, other applications, users, enterprise policy)
- Allows Architecture Review Team to proactively recognize when modifications to the architecture are required
- Allows the project team to provide input to the extension of the proposed architecture
- Allows the project to leverage existing common services where applicable
- Provides cost effectiveness across the enterprise

### *Architecture Assurance Methodology*

The Architecture Assurance Group is a multidisciplinary body that is responsible for the maintenance and enforcement of Architecture, Design standards and best practices across the programs/projects. The primary responsibility is to provide governance and ensure compliance of the defined enterprise / solution architecture.

Architecture Assurance is the key success factor in ensuring high quality deliverables for the architecture and design phases. The intent of the Architecture Assurance Process is to ensure that ongoing projects have the right architectural assumptions and that in-flight projects receive architectural guidance throughout the life cycle. This should be a collaborative effort to ensure that project designs and implementations are compliant with the defined architecture. A detailed Architecture Assurance process that achieves these goals and solution fitment is shown below:

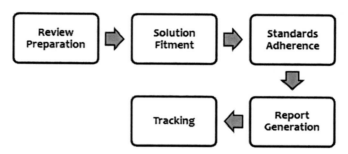

*Architecture Assurance Methodology*

Step 1: Review Preparation
- Ensure Completeness in terms of coverage and sufficiency of submitted artefacts

Step 2: Solution Fitment / Functional Fitment
- Non-Functional Fitment
- Completeness of design with regard to requirements
- Options and design decisions

Step 3: Standards Adherence
- Alignment with architecture requirements
- Alignment with architecture principles
- Alignment with IT Strategy
- Exception and Approval

Step 4: Report Generation
- Review report with regard to business, data, application & technology
- Finding & Observations
- Gaps & Issues

Step 5: Tracking
- Presenting the report to stakeholders
- Tracking observations to closure
- Oversee updated architecture artefacts

## Review Preparation

Architecture/Design Review(s) should be conducted at a stage when there is still time to correct any major inconsistencies or shortcomings in the program/project.

The Architecture/Design Review is typically targeted for the Analysis SDLC phase and at a point in time when:

- Business goals, business requirements, policies are defined
- Ballpark clarity of hardware and software requirements and decisions are not finalized
- Project schedules / timelines are defined
- Project risk assessment is done

Architecture Review Criteria is:

- Start Early
- Drive and Participate in architecture workshop
- Establish relationship with architecture and design teams
- Involve (who?) through architecture and design
- Involve and review the architecture and design decisions on an ongoing basis
- Review the intermittent and final architecture deliverables
- Share architecture best practices
- Mentor architecture and design teams as appropriate
- Architectural Risk Analysis and Mitigation
- Quality attribute analysis of architecture
- Failure and risk analysis of architecture
- Mentor on engineering best practices
- Mentor on Development method, tools and build practices
- Performance and other NFR related best practices

During the review, the architecture review team needs to extract the information like impacted groups, impacted systems, data feeds, software components required such as build, buy and reuse, security requirement, availability, scalability, error handling, capacity sizing, integration with third parties, data center/hosting facility, etc.

Key activities of the Architecture Assurance Group are:

- Conduct planned and random formal architecture review workshops for projects and programs
- Analyze architecture quality attributes against requirements
- Conduct architecture failure and risk analysis and mitigation plan
- Identify areas of non-compliance and options to redress shortcomings
- Conduct formal/informal reviews of intermediate and final architecture deliverables to ensure ongoing compliance and quality
- Review and track architecture and design decisions

**Solution Fitment**

In this phase, Architecture Assurance looks for a high-level functional fit and nonfunctional fitment of the solution. Also verifies the solution mapping with the design and various options provided for the solution, reasons for the choices, TCO analysis of each option, etc.

**Standards Adherence**

In this phase, the verification of the alignment of the solution with the architecture requirements is done. Proper realization of the Architecture Principles, Architecture Patterns, and IT Strategy alignment is performed in this phase. Any deviation of the standards needs to be approved by the Architecture Assurance Group.

## Report Preparation

In this phase, the report will be reviewed in terms of business, data, application and technology. Also, identification of the open items, action items and next steps will be addressed and communicated to the project team.

## Tracking

The prepared report will be presented to the program management and the observations to the closure are tracked. In this Phase, we oversee the updated architecture artifacts.

### *Architecture Review Process*

To ensure smooth, timely, and low impact reviews, the involved parties should prepare within the guidelines below. The process flow is shown in the following figure.

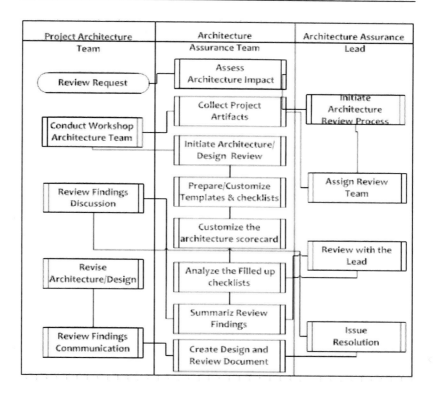

*Architecture Review Process*

The project architecture team is responsible for:
- Developing a project description that provides sufficient detail for the review team to evaluate architectural risks, including the project size, business impact, NFRs, Architecture Principles
- Sharing project estimates

The Architecture Assurance Team is responsible for:
- Assessing projects for architectural impact during the Proposal/Project Initiation phase of the SDLC processes

- Providing guidance to projects through the design phase to ensure that the final design is architecturally compliant
- Prepare/Customize Architecture Templates, Architecture Checklist
- Participate in the Architecture Review meetings to provide support to project teams and to assist the Architecture Assurance Group in decision making.
- Analyze the filled up Checklist, Summarize the review findings
- Customize Architecture Metrics

As part of the Architecture Review Process the following standards of the system need to be reviewed and agreed to.

**Business:**
- Business Strategy, Goals & Vision
- IT Strategy
- Existing Budgets, Resource Plans, Project Plans
- Business Scope Description
- Use Case Specification
- Business Requirements Document (BRD)
- Service Level Agreements
- TCO Model (CAPEX/OPEX etc.) - Funding Status
- Build/Buy/Reuse(Retrofit) Considerations
- Business process modeling and workflow system
- Business Process Optimization
- Business Process Analysis
- Business Process Monitoring & SLA's

**Application:**
- Application platform
- Programming/scripting language
- Testing/monitoring tools
- User interface platform

98

- Enterprise application integration platform
- Conceptual Architecture
- Logical Architecture
- Physical Architecture
- Security Architecture
- Portal platform
- Architecture Frameworks
- Performance Tuning Plan
- Migration Plan
- Tool/Vendor Selection Results

**Data:**
- Data Strategy
- Logical Data Model (LDM)
- Physical Data Model (PDM)
- Data integration platform
- Reporting and data analysis platform

**Infrastructure:**
- Server platform and operating system
- Desktop platform and operating system
- Bill of Materials
- H/W & S/W Acquisition/Lease Plan
- Security Implementation/Management Plan
- Deployment Plan
- Operational Readiness Plan
- Release Plan
- Network infrastructure
- System Performance Report
- Disaster Recovery Plan

The Architecture Assurance Lead will perform the following activities:
- Assign Review Team
- Disagreement/Issue Resolution

- Review Findings discussion and agreement & communication with the project/program team

Review members will:
- Commit to review all materials in advance
- Prepare detailed questions using this practice standard and Checklist as appropriate
- Conduct any preliminary research as necessary to be an informed team member
- Attend all review meetings
- Provide a final assessment and recommendation based on their interpretation of the impact of the proposed solution architecture and design on the Enterprise Architecture.

### *Summary*

One of the most important truths about the architecture of a system is it will tell you important properties of the system itself, even if the system does not yet exist. Architects make design decisions because of the downstream effects they will have on the system(s) they are building, and these effects are known and predictable. If they were not, the process of crafting architecture would be no better than throwing dice. We would pick an architecture at random, build a system from it, see if the system had the desired properties and if not, and go back to the drawing board. While architecture is not yet a cookbook science, we know we can do much better than random guessing.

An effective technique to assess a candidate architecture before it becomes the project's accepted blueprint is of great economic value. With the advent of repeatable, structured methods, architecture evaluation has come to provide a relatively low cost risk mitigation capability. An architecture evaluation should be a standard part of every architecture based development methodology.

It is almost always cost effective to evaluate software quality as early as possible in the life cycle. If problems are found early, they are easier to correct; a change to a requirement, specification, or design is all that is necessary. Software quality cannot be appended late in a project, but must be inherent from the beginning, built in by design. It is in the project's best interest for prospective candidate designs to be evaluated (and rejected, if necessary) during the design phase, before long-term institutionalization.

However, architecture evaluation can be carried out at many points during a system's life cycle. If the architecture is still embryonic, you can evaluate those decisions that have already been made or are being considered. You can choose among architectural alternatives. If the architecture is finished, or nearly so, you can validate it before the project commits to lengthy and expensive development. It also makes sense to evaluate the architecture of a legacy system that is undergoing modification, porting, integration with other systems, or other significant upgrades. Finally, architecture evaluation makes an excellent discovery vehicle. Development projects often need to understand how an inherited system meets (or whether it meets) its quality attributes requirements.

# 8. Measuring ROI for EA Transformation

This chapter illustrates useful techniques for estimating the return on investment or ROI of enterprise architecture. The use of the enterprise architecture results in better, faster, and cheaper information technology, which satisfies organizational goals and objectives. This chapter also provides an overview of enterprise architecture, along with its relevant background and organizing frameworks. It provides useful metrics and models, an exposition of its costs and benefits, and a detailed return on investment analysis. Finally, it concludes with useful principles for successful enterprise architecture and return on investment.

## Introduction

The impact of enterprise architecture can be measured using six metrics: (a) costs, (b) benefits, (c) benefit to cost ratio, (d) return on investment, (e) net present value, and (f) breakeven point. Costs are simply the accumulation of expenses, such as labor, training, tools, creating the various models, verification and validation, and compliance or maturity assessment. Benefits are the monetization of increased operational efficiency, reduced operational costs and personnel numbers, increased customer satisfaction, and consolidated legacy computer systems. Historically, organizations are notoriously irresponsible when it comes to keeping track of costs. And, benefits are a little more challenging to identify and monetize.

| Costs | Total amount of Money Spend on Enterprise Architecture |
|---|---|
| Benefits | Total amount of Money gained from Enterprise Architecture |
| Benefit to Cost Ratio | Ratio of Enterprise Architecture Benefits to Cost |
| ROI % | Ratio of adjusted Enterprise Architecture Benefits to Cost |
| Net Present Value | Discounted Cash Flows of Enterprise Architecture |
| Break Even Point | Point where Benefits exceeds costs of Enterprise Architecture |

### Costs and Benefits

There are also five major classes of costs and benefits for enterprise architecture: (a) financial improvement, (b) constituent services, (c) reduced redundancy, (d) economic development, and (e) fostering democracy. Financial improvements mean reducing the costs of organizations and enhancing revenue collection. Constituent services mean improved service to customers, suppliers, and key stakeholders. Reduced redundancy means consolidating, reducing, or eliminating unnecessary legacy computer systems. Economic development means to grow local, state, and federal economies. Finally, fostering democracy may mean offering a consistent level of customer service to all stakeholders, regardless of political affiliation. Unfortunately, few organizations consistently collect cost and benefit data, and certainly not according to a standard.

103

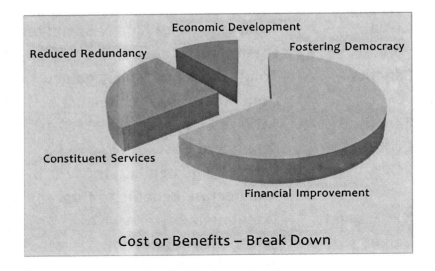

Cost or Benefits – Break Down

## *Principles for Successful Return on Investment*

The return on investment principles go hand in hand with the tips, tricks, and techniques for enterprise architecture. Some people feel measuring payback is a principle for the industrial age and some believe it is a path towards the 21st Century. Some say return on investment is irrelevant in lieu of net present value, and the plethora of payback algorithms. The bottom line is that return on investment is a strategic approach to measuring the value of any activity, especially enterprise architecture.

The goal of enterprise architecture is to enable an organization to realize its strategic goals and objectives by streamlining its information technology infrastructure. And, strategic plans are simply a means of ensuring the operational efficiency and effectiveness of organizations and firms alike. The problem is that few people apply return on investment, and few apply it in a consistent manner. The way to avoid this is to elevate return on investment to center stage, identify measurable goals and objectives, and strive to achieve them in every way. The fact is, enterprise architecture, information technology, and return on investment are intimately and intricately linked, and are insufficient by themselves.

### Use ROI as a success factor

Use return on investment to drive enterprise architecture. By definition, the goal of enterprise architecture is to align an organization's strategy with its information technology. By implication, a strategy cannot be realized without this alignment. Set out to measure the costs and benefits of using enterprise architecture for this alignment:

*Etch the desired benefits in stone:* Identify a core set of benefits that you wish to realize from enterprise architecture. Establish measurable goals for operating efficiency, cost reductions, staff reductions, customer satisfaction, computing budgets, and economic growth. Monetize the benefits early (e.g., convert improvements into money), which many don't do.

*Establish early ROI objectives:* Establish ambitious return on investment objectives for enterprise architecture based on tangible measures of costs and benefits. Use return on investment to establish safety margins. That is, given the risk of any project or initiative, ensure the payoff far exceeds the cost of enterprise architecture, lest you end up with none.

*Operationalize a core set of metrics:* Define a set of clear, measurable, and quantitative economic benefits for enterprise architecture. Examples include people, time, budgets, customers, throughput, volume, bandwidth, computers, and maintenance. Common mistakes are failing to define metrics, defining qualitative ones, or defining far too many metrics.

*Continuously measure the payback:* Measure the return on investment of enterprise architecture early and frequently. Measure the payback at regular intervals along with normal project management activities, such as cost, time, and earned value reporting. Payback can be estimated similarly to cost and schedule performance inices before it's too late.

*Use automated tools to do the work:* Use an integrated project management reporting system with built-in return on investment tracking and reporting. There's no sense in having to master all of the latest payback formulas or designating a return on investment manager. Instead, collect payback data automatically and have the computer system help you along.

*Standardize ROI reporting:* Create a system for measuring and reporting measures for the return on investment of enterprise architecture. It's virtually impossible to do so with so many existing local, state, federal, and international enterprise architecture initiatives. It's just too difficult to measure payback after the fact without a standard system in place.

### Summary
This chapter covered several useful topics in enterprise architecture which are closely related. First, enterprise architecture was introduced, it identified who was doing enterprise architecture and why, and its organizing framework was described. Then, simple metrics and models for return on investment were introduced, the benefits of enterprise architecture were described, and return on investment data were presented from real world initiatives. Finally, detailed principles for successful enterprise architecture and return on investment were discussed.

The goal of enterprise architecture is to improve the operational efficiency and effectiveness of organizations by aligning their strategies with their information technology. And, return on investment is an excellent way to measure the success or failure of enterprise architecture. It is essential to introduce and describe the goals and objectives of enterprise architecture before introducing and describing how to measure payback, because they are so closely related.

Metrics and models come next, to establish the context and set the stage for how to measure the return on investment of enterprise architecture. From this, we observe that the fundamental elements of measuring payback are costs and benefits, and return on investment flows naturally from these.

The most challenging aspect of measuring the payback of enterprise architecture is to identify, measure, and monetize its economic benefits. The most labor intensive part of this approach is to broach the subject of how to clearly identify the benefits.

# 9. Reference Architecture and Frameworks

Reference architecture provides needed architectural information that can be provided in advance to an enterprise to enable consistent architectural best practices. Enterprise Reference Architecture helps business owners to actualize their strategies, vision, objectives, and principles. It evaluates the IT systems, based on Reference Architecture goals, principles, and standards. It helps to reduce IT costs by increasing functionality, availability, scalability, etc. Telecom Reference Architecture provides customers with the flexibility to view bundled service bills online with the provision of multiple services. It provides real-time, flexible billing and charging systems, to handle complex promotions, discounts, and settlements with multiple parties. This chapter attempts to describe the Reference Architecture for the Telecom Enterprises. It lays the foundation for a Telecom Reference Architecture by articulating the requirements, drivers, and pitfalls for telecom service providers. It describes generic reference architecture for telecom enterprises.

A Reference Architecture provides a methodology, set of practices, template, and standards based on a set of successful solutions implemented earlier. These solutions have been generalized and structured for the depiction of both a logical and a physical architecture, based on the harvesting of a set of patterns that describe observations in a number of successful implementations. It helps as a reference for the various architectures that an enterprise can implement to solve various problems. It can be used as the starting point or the point of comparisons for various departments or business entities of a company, or alternately for the various companies and enterprise. It provides multiple views for multiple stakeholders. Major artifacts of the Enterprise Reference Architecture are methodologies, standards, metadata, documents, design patterns, etc.

### *Purpose of Reference Architecture*

In most cases, architects spend a lot of time researching, investigating, defining, and re-arguing architectural decisions. It is like reinventing the wheel as their peers in other organizations or even the same organization have already spent a lot of time and effort defining their own architectural practices. This prevents an organization from learning from its own experiences and applying that knowledge for increased effectiveness. Reference architecture provides missing architectural information that can be provided in advance to project team members to enable consistent architectural best practices. Enterprise Reference Architecture helps an enterprise to achieve the following at the abstract level:

- Reference architecture is more of a communication channel to an enterprise
- Helps the business owners to accommodate to their strategies, vision, objectives, and principles
- Evaluates the IT systems based on Reference Architecture Principles
- Reduces IT spending through increasing functionality, availability, scalability, etc.
- A Real-time Integration Model helps to reduce the latency of the data updates
- Is used to define a single source of Information
- Provides a clear view on how to manage information and security

- Defines the policy around the data ownership, product boundaries, etc.
- Helps with cost optimization across project and solution portfolios by eliminating unused or duplicate investments and assets
- Has a shorter implementation time and cost

Once the reference architecture is in place, the set of architectural principles, standards, reference models, and best practices ensure that the aligned investments have the greatest possible likelihood of success in both the near term and the long term (TCO).

***Common pitfalls for Telecom Service Providers***
Telecom Reference Architecture serves as the first step towards maturity for a telecom service Provider. During the course of our assignments/experiences with telecom players, we have come across the following observations – Some of these indicate a lack of maturity of the telecom service provider:
- In markets that are growing and not so mature, it has been observed that telcos have a significant amount of in-house or home-grown applications. In some of these markets, the growth has been so rapid that IT has been unable to cope with business demands. Telcos have shown a tendency to come up with workarounds in their IT applications so as to meet business needs.
- Even for core functions like provisioning or mediation, some telcos have tried to manage with home-grown applications.
- Most of the applications do not have the required scalability or maintainability to sustain growth in volumes or functionality.
- Applications face interoperability issues with other applications in the operator's landscape. Integrat-

ing a new application or network element requires considerable effort on the part of the other applications.

- Application boundaries are not clear, and functionality that is not in the initial scope of that application gets pushed onto it. This results in the development of the multiple, small applications without proper boundaries.
- Usage of Legacy OSS/BSS systems, poor Integration across Multiple COTS Products and Internal Systems. Most of the Integrations are developed on ad-hoc basis and Point-to-Point Integration.
- Redundancy of the business functions in different applications
- Fragmented data across the different applications and no integrated view of the strategic data
- Lot of performance Issues due to the usage of the complex integration across OSS and BSS systems

However, this is where the maturity of the telecom industry as a whole can be of help. The collaborative efforts of telcos to overcome some of these problems have resulted in bodies like the TM Forum. They have come up with frameworks for business processes, data, applications, and technology for telecom service providers. These could be a good starting point for telcos to clean up their enterprise landscape.

### Drivers of Reference Architecture

The drivers of the Reference Architecture are Reference Architecture Goals, Principles, and Enterprise Vision and Telecom Transformation. The details are depicted in the diagram below.

Today's telecom reference architectures should seamlessly integrate traditional legacy-based applications and transition to next-generation network technologies (e.g., IP multimedia subsystems). This has resulted in new requirements for flexible, real-time billing and OSS/BSS systems and implications on the service provider's organizational requirements and structure.

Telecom reference architectures are today expected to:

- Integrate voice, messaging, email and other VAS over fixed and mobile networks and back end systems
- Be able to provision multiple services and service bundles
- Deliver converged voice, video and data services
- Leverage the existing Network Infrastructure
- Provide real-time, flexible billing and charging systems to handle complex promotions, discounts, and settlements with multiple parties.
- Support charging of advanced data services such as VoIP, On-Demand, Services (e.g. Video), IMS/SIP Services, Mobile Money, Content Services and IPTV
- Help in faster deployment of new services
- Serve as an effective platform for collaboration between network IT and business organizations
- Harness the potential of converging technology, networks, devices and content to develop multimedia services and solutions of ever-increasing sophistication on a single Internet Protocol (IP)
- Ensure better service delivery and zero revenue leakage through real-time balance and credit management
- Lower operating costs to drive profitability

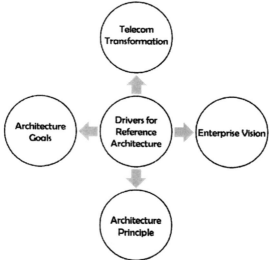

*Drivers for Reference Architecture*

## Telecom Transformation
- Ever-increasing subscriber expectations
- Need to retain existing subscribers
- Pressure to maximize ARPU and profile per user
- Increasing complexity of telecom services due to convergence
- Pressure to decrease Time-to-market
- Need to be compatible with other products and vendor

## Enterprise Vision
- Be flexible to changing business needs
- Ensure customer satisfaction
- Be adaptable to changes in technology

## Architecture Principles
- Technology Neutrality
- Parsimony
- Loose coupling of models

- Applicability
- Architecture Goals
- SOA based service integration
- Enable Service Visibility
- Handle growing complexity
- Enable interactions between models
- Enable better governance and performance
- Cross Ownership Boundaries

### Enterprise Reference Architecture

The Enterprise Reference Architecture (RA) fills the gap between the concepts and vocabulary defined by the reference model and the implementation. Reference architecture provides detailed architectural information in a common format such that solutions can be repeatedly designed and deployed in a consistent, high-quality, supportable fashion. This chapter attempts to describe the Reference Architecture for the Telecom Application Usage and how to achieve the Enterprise Level Reference Architecture using SOA.

- Telecom Reference Architecture
- Enterprise SOA based Reference Architecture


### Telecom Reference Architecture

Tele Management Forum's New Generation Operations Systems and Software (NGOSS) is an architectural framework for organizing, integrating, and implementing telecom systems. NGOSS is a component-based framework consisting of the following elements:

- The enhanced Telecom Operations Map (eTOM) is a business process framework.
- The Shared Information Data (SID) model provides a comprehensive information framework that may be specialized for the needs of a particular organization.

- The Telecom Application Map (TAM) is an application framework to depict the functional footprint of applications, relative to the horizontal processes within eTOM.
- The Technology Neutral Architecture (TNA) is an integrated framework. TNA is an architecture that is sustainable through technology changes.

NGOSS Architecture Standards are Centralized data:
- Loosely coupled distributed systems
- Application components/re-use
- A technology-neutral system framework with technology specific implementations
- Interoperability to service provider data/processes
- Allows more re-use of business components across multiple business scenarios
- Workflow automation

The traditional operator systems architecture consists of four layers,
- Business Support System (BSS) layer, with focus toward customers and business partners. Manages order, subscriber, pricing, rating, and billing information.
- Operations Support System (OSS) layer, built around product, service, and resource inventories.
- Networks layer – consists of Network elements and 3rd Party Systems.
- Integration Layer – to maximize application communication and overall solution flexibility.

The reference architecture for telecom enterprises is depicted below.

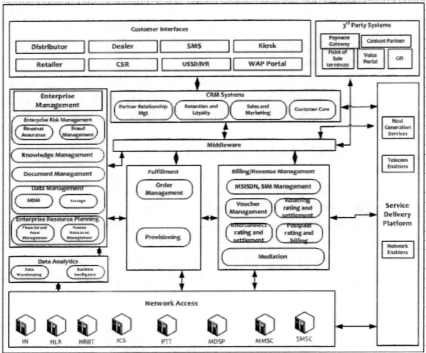

*Telecom Reference Architecture*

## Frameworks

### Telecom

- *eTOM:* The Business Process Framework (eTOM), published by the TM Forum, is a guidebook that defines the most widely used and accepted standard for business processes in the telecommunications industry. The Business Process Framework model describes the full scope of business processes required by a service provider and defines key elements and how they interact.
- Business Process Framework is a common companion of ITIL, an analogous standard or framework for best practices in information technology.

116

Both of these frameworks are part of the larger context of Total Quality Management, in which many industries have, since 1950, increasingly formalized their business processes and metrics in search of higher quality, fewer defects, and greater efficiency. ISO 9000 is probably the best known of these "process and results improvement" standards, but it is far more generic than either business process management framework or ITIL.

- The Business Process Framework model consists of Level-0, Level-1, Level-2, Level-3 and Level-4 processes. These levels form a hierarchy, with each level encapsulating a group of processes at the next level of detail. The graphic representation of a Business Process Framework model consists of rows and columns, the intersections of which denote specific business processes. The top row includes customer facing activities such as marketing, while the bottom row includes supplier facing and support activities. In this manner the Business Process Framework map covers the whole value chain. The map also indicates the interaction between processes.

- Business Process Framework processes fall into three broad sections: "Strategy, Infrastructure & Product," "Operations," and "Enterprise Management."

- *TAM:* The TM Forum Applications Framework is produced by the TM Forum. The TM Forum is the world's industry association of web, telecom and media companies focused on end-to-end service management. The TM Forum's Frameworx is a comprehensive, integrated set of tools for defining, developing, procuring and deploying operational and business support systems and software. The scope covers the complete OSS / BSS development lifecycle.

- Frameworx comprises a packaged set of industry agreed guidelines, maps, models, methodologies, specifications, a developers' toolkit and standardized interface definitions to guide the definition, development, procurement, and deployment of interoperable OSS/BSS solutions. These Frameworx artifacts, and the clearly defined methodology for using them, assist the user to define, design and build Frameworx solutions that can easily integrate into any Frameworx compliant environment.

- The TM Forum Applications Framework or the TAM (Telecom Application Map) is one of the primary Frameworx artifacts. It considers the role and the functionality of the various applications that deliver OSS (Operations Support System) and BSS (Business Support System) capability. Structured along similar lines to other TM Forum artifacts, the business process framework (eTOM) and the information framework (SID), it is presented in a similar layered and vertical structure.

- *SID:* Shared Information/Data Model or SID is a unified reference data model providing a single set of terms for business objects in telecommunications. The objective is to enable people in different departments, companies or geographical locations to use the same terms to describe the same real world objects, practices and relationships. The Tele Management Forum's Frameworx Shared Information/Data (SID) model provides the telecommunications industry with a common vocabulary and set of information/data definitions and relationships used in the definition of NGOSS architectures, now known as Frameworx. The SID is an ob-

118

ject model, which uses Unified Modeling Language (UML), a data and process modeling language, to define entities and define the relationships between them, as well as the attributes and processes (termed methods) which make up the entity or object.

- SID, as the Frameworx information model, provides an information/data reference model and a common information/data vocabulary from a business, as well as, a systems perspective. The SID uses UML to formalize the expression of the needs of a particular stakeholder viewpoint.

- SID provides the common language for communicating the concerns of the four major groups of constituents (stakeholders) represented by the Viewpoints: Business, System, Implementation and Deployment, as defined in the NGOSS Lifecycle. Used in combination with the eTOM business process and activity descriptions and the Telecom Application Map (TAM) the SID acts as a bridge between the business and Information Technology groups within an organization by providing definitions that are understandable by the business, but are also rigorous enough to be used for software development.

## Oil and Gas

Energistics is a global industry consortium that facilitates an inclusive user community for the development, adoption and maintenance of collaborative, open standards for the energy industry in general and specifically for oil and gas exploration and production.

Energistics encourages the industry to use open standards, delivers business value to the upstream oil and natural gas industry through business process efficiencies across the entire exploration and production life cycle. Energistics is a membership organization. The work of the consortium concentrates on helping upstream oil and natural gas companies through the development, support, and promotion of standards that address data definition, handling, storage, and exchange in the context of technology, computing, communications, and business processes.

Some of the industry standards that Energistics endorses or maintains correspond to major subject areas of oil and gas exploration and production, while others are generally applicable across the industry.

## Defense

The DoDAF - Department of Defense Architecture Framework provides a foundational framework for developing and representing architecture descriptions that ensure a common denominator for understanding, comparing, and integrating architectures across organizational, joint, and multinational boundaries. It establishes data element definitions, rules, and relationships and a baseline set of products for consistent development of systems, integrated, or federated architectures. These architecture descriptions may include families of systems (FoS), systems of systems (SoS), and net centric capabilities for interoperating and interacting in the non-combat environment.

All major U.S. DoD weapons and information technology system acquisitions are required to develop and document an enterprise architecture (EA) using the views prescribed in the DoDAF. While it is clearly aimed at military systems, DoDAF has broad applicability across the private, public and voluntary sectors around the world, and represents one of a large number of systems architecture frameworks.

The purpose of DoDAF is to define concepts and models usable in DoD's six core processes:
- Joint Capabilities Integration and Development (JCIDS)
- Planning, Programming, Budgeting and Execution (PPBE)
- Defense Acquisition System (DAS)
- Systems Engineering (SE)
- Operational Planning (OPLAN)
- Capability Portfolio Management (CPM)

**Retail**

The Association for Retail Technology Standards (ARTS) Data Model is the information standard in the retail industry, containing 650 tables with more than 4,500 fully defined data elements. With contributions spanning over the last 15 years, the Model encompasses all key segments of retail, including: merchandising, inventory, ordering, reports, workforce, CRM and POS, therefore providing the data architecture to organize the entire retail enterprise. Designed to help simplify the industry, the Data Model is a single source of consistent and accurate information, providing vendors and retailers a common standard on which to build flexible solutions that are easily modified to accommodate business change. Application developers who have adopted the Data Model (such as Retail Anywhere) use it as a base for application development, add their own functionalities and create a unique user interface. Developers using the established Data Model allow retailers to choose proven, best of breed solutions.

**Pipeline**

The PODS Pipeline Data Model provides the database that architecture pipeline operators use to store critical information and analysis data about their pipeline systems, and manage this data geospatially in a linear referenced database, which can then be visualized in any GIS platform. The PODS Pipeline Data Model houses the asset information, inspection, integrity management, regulatory compliance, risk analysis, history and operational data that pipeline companies have deemed mission critical to the successful management of natural gas and hazardous liquids pipelines.

Typical information stored in a PODS database includes (partial list): centerline location, pipeline materials and coatings, MAOP, valves and pipeline components, catholic protection facilities and inspection results, hydrotesting, operating conditions, physical inspection results, leak detection surveys, repairs, foreign line crossings, inline inspection (ILI) results, close interval survey results, pump and compression equipment specifications, geographic boundaries, external records, risk analysis methods and results, regulatory reports, and pipeline and ROW maintenance activities, among others.

**Petroleum**

The Professional Petroleum Data Management Association (PPDM Association) is a global, not-for-profit organization that works collaboratively within the petroleum industry to create and promote standards and best practices for data management. The Association's vision is the global adoption of data management standards and best practices throughout the upstream (exploration and production) petroleum industry.

The PPDM Model is suitable for a master data management system. The specifications DDL are provided for use in Oracle and SQL Server systems. In addition, the modular design allows selected portions to be used in business specific databases and applications.

Although it was originally called a public model, it was never freely distributed by the Association. "Public" always meant "non-proprietary" not "free." The way to get the Model is to become a member of the Association. However, many non-members around the world continue to use versions or adaptations of the PPDM model, usually because the model is embedded in a database or application purchased from a software provider. PPDM Lite, a simplified model based on Version 3.7, is available free to any registered user on the PPDM website.

The PPDM Model is a set of specifications for creating a relational database. It is not a set of data for the petroleum industry. By analogy, the model is only the blueprint for a huge pigeon loft (birdhouse); it does not have birds in the pigeon holes. However, the Model contains a vast amount of knowledge about the industry's business practices (how the data are acquired and used.) The Association estimates that Version 3.8 represents over $100 million of invested funds and human resources since inception.

## Banking

Many banking industry participants including the founding members of The Banking Industry Architecture Network (BIAN) have frequently observed a common and enduring problem: excessive complexity in most Banks' application portfolios. This complexity results in inflexible/unresponsive systems, inflated enhancement, maintenance and operational costs; and an inability to leverage rapidly evolving advanced solutions, technologies, approaches and business models.

BIAN set out to address this issue by developing a common industry standard to define functional partitions and service operations that could be used inside any bank with the anticipated benefits already noted. However, the BIAN objective raises a key question: why should the BIAN model and approach be any better than previous attempts to address application portfolio complexity?

At the core of BIAN's proposition is the adoption of a service oriented approach to architecting the systems that support the bank. This approach is fundamentally different from the prevailing 'process–centric' designs. To underscore this critical difference, a comparison can be made with architectural disciplines when applied to the highly tangible problem of designing the layout of a city, as opposed to the much less tangible design of a commercial enterprise such as a bank.

Any design is a combination of the ingredients that are used and the behaviors that the design is intended to support. The ingredients relate to static or persistent things that are "deployed" and the behaviors refer to more dynamic patterns of desired responses to anticipated events or triggers. An architect understanding how the ingredients need to be configured to support the intended behaviors will develop an efficient overall design. In the case of the city designer, this is a town plan. The ingredients seen in the town plan are the buildings, parks and communications infrastructure that need to be in place to support the anticipated behaviors of the town's inhabitants. These behaviors could be traced as journeys or "days in the life" of a town plan.

## Insurance

The ACORD Framework is an industry standard reference architecture. It is an enterprise view of the insurance industry with an accounting of business functions (e.g. capabilities) and the related business concepts that support those functions. The reference models that comprise the Framework can be utilized individually or collectively. The Framework is not an "all or nothing" architecture. Its use depends on your business objectives and what you are trying to achieve. The ACORD Framework is comprised of the following:

- Business Glossary
- Capability Model
- Information Model
- Data Model
- Component Mode

*The Business Glossary* contains common business terms with definitions found within the insurance domain. It can be utilized to bridge communication gaps and provides context across all business areas. It contains more than 3,100 business terms.

*The Capability Model* defines what the insurance industry does and serves as the baseline of a company's capabilities. Its scope begins with insurance companies, but is not limited to insurers. The capabilities exist in the industry, regardless of whether one company performs all of them.

*The Information Model* organizes, explains, and relates insurance concepts. It is a single model and provides a "big picture" view of the industry. This model is about concepts, not literal implementations. It can express ideas independently of how they are used and is not intended to describe how to use the concepts. It is designed for extensibility to accommodate industry requirements. Its view is context-neutral or context-agnostic ("data at rest").

*The Data Model* is generated from the Information Model to provide content alignment and traceability, and also ensures the two models are always synchronized. The Data Model makes the abstract more tangible by turning concepts from Information Model into a format that can be used for persistence (e.g. storage). Uses of the data model include: helping create a physical data model for databases, providing a baseline for data warehouses, validating your data model.

*The Component Model* is the marriage of capabilities and information. It defines a design framework that allows for the independent development of components that interoperate to form applications. It uses technology neutral interfaces allowing for implementation across development platforms. With this design a single component is reusable across multiple applications and interchangeable with other components.

### Summary

A Reference Architecture provides a methodology, set of practices, template and standards based on a collection of successful solutions implemented earlier. These solutions have been generalized and structured for the depiction of both a logical and a physical architecture, based on the harvesting of a set of patterns that describe observations in a number of successful implementations. It serves as a reference for the distinct architectures that an enterprise can implement to solve various problems. It can be used as the starting point or the point of comparisons for differing departments and business entities of a company, or for the various companies of an enterprise. It provides multiple views for multiple stakeholders. Major artifacts of the Enterprise Reference Architecture are methodologies, standards, metadata, documents, design patterns, etc.

In most cases, architects spend a lot of time researching, investigating, defining, and re-arguing architectural decisions. It is like reinventing the wheel as their peers in other organizations or even the same organization have already spent a lot of time and effort defining their own architectural practices. This prevents an organization from learning from its own experiences and applying that knowledge for increased effectiveness. Reference architecture provides missing architectural information that can be provided in advance to project team members to enable consistent architectural best practices

Once the reference architecture is in place, the set of architectural principles, standards, reference models, and best practices ensure that the aligned investments have the greatest possible likelihood of success in both the near term and the long term (TCO).

Reference models provide an enterprise, or a class of enterprises such as an entire industry, with a recommendation for structuring. The telecommunications industry has eTOM, for example. TOGAF is also a reference model, as are ITIL and Cobit.

The Enterprise Reference Architecture helps business owners to actualize their strategies, vision, objectives, and principles while enabling consistent architectural best practices – building the structure that supports the industry.

# 10. EA Frameworks

An architecture framework is a tool that can be used for developing a broad range of architectures. An architecture framework describes a method for designing an information system in terms of a set of building blocks and for showing how the building blocks fit together. A framework contains a set of tools and provides a common vocabulary. A framework also includes a list of recommended standards and compliant products that can be used to implement the building blocks.

## *Need for a Framework for Enterprise Architecture*

Using an architecture framework will speed up and simplify architecture development, ensure more complete coverage of the designed solution, and make certain that the architecture selected allows for future growth in response to the needs of the business.

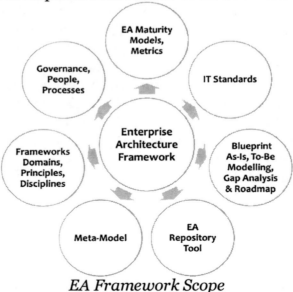

*EA Framework Scope*

128

## *Leveraging Frameworks for EA Transformation*

Many enterprise architectural methodologies have come and gone in the last 20 years. At this point, perhaps 90 percent of the field use one of these four methodologies:

- The Zachman Framework for Enterprise Architectures—A taxonomy
- The Open Group Architectural Framework (TOGAF)—A process
- The Federal Enterprise Architecture—Implemented enterprise architecture or a proscriptive methodology
- The Gartner Methodology—Enterprise architectural practice

This chapter both outlines these common methodologies and proposes another approach, one that is a blended methodology. Therefore, an organization can choose bits and pieces from each of these methodologies, and modify and merge them according to the specific needs of the organization.

A blended methodology will only be as good as an organization's commitment to making changes. This commitment must be driven by the highest level of the organization. With a real commitment to change, and a tailored methodology for guiding that change, the promise of enterprise architecture is within reach.

## *Zachman Framework for Enterprise Architectures*

The Zachman Framework is actually a taxonomy for organizing architectural artifacts (in other words, design documents, specifications, and models) that takes into account i) who the artifact targets (for example, business owner and builder) and ii) what particular

129

issue (for example, data and functionality) is being addressed.

As John Zachman retrospectively described his work: "The Framework as it applies to Enterprises is simply a logical structure for classifying and organizing the descriptive representations of an Enterprise that are significant to the management of the Enterprise as well as to the development of the Enterprise's systems." The Zachman Framework as it is portrayed today is shown below.

| | What (Data) | How (Function) | Where (Locations) | Who (People) | When (Time) | Why (Motivation) |
|---|---|---|---|---|---|---|
| **Scope (Planner)** | List of things important to the business | List of processes that the business performs | List of locations important to the business | List of organizations important to the business | List of events/cycles important to the business | List of business goals / strategies |
| **Business Model (Business owner)** | Semantic Model | Business Process Model | Business Logistics System | Workflow Model | Master Schedule | Business Plan |
| **System Model (Designer)** | Logical Data Model | Application Architecture | Distributed System Architecture | Human Interface Architecture | Process Structure | Business Rules Model |
| **Technology Model (Implementer)** | Physical Data Model | System Design | Technology Architecture | Presentation Architecture | Control Structure | Rule Design |
| **Detailed Representation (Subcontractor)** | Data Definition | Program | Network Architecture | Security Architecture | Timing Definition | Rule Definition |
| **Functional Areas (Functioning system)** | Data | Function | Network | Organization | Schedule | Strategy |

*Zachman Framework*

As you can see in the figure, there are 36 intersecting cells in a Zachman grid, one for each meeting point between a player's perspective (for example, business owner) and a descriptive focus (for example, data). As we move horizontally in the grid, we see different descriptions of the system—all from the same player's perspective. As we move vertically in the grid, we see a single focus, that of the player from whose perspective we are viewing that focus.

The first suggestion of the Zachman taxonomy is that every architectural artifact should live in one and only one cell. There should be no ambiguity about where a particular artifact lives. If it is not clear in which cell a particular artifact lives, there is most likely a problem with the artifact itself.

The second suggestion of the Zachman taxonomy is that architecture can be considered a complete architecture only when every cell in that architecture is complete. A cell is complete when it contains sufficient artifacts to fully define the system for one specific player looking at one specific descriptive focus. When every cell is populated with appropriate artifacts, there is a sufficient amount of detail to fully describe the system from the perspective of every player (what we might today call a stakeholder) looking at the system from every possible angle.

The third suggestion of the Zachman grid is that cells in columns should be related to each other. Consider, for example, the data column (the first column) of the Zachman grid. From the business owner's perspective, data is information about the business. From the database administrator's perspective, data is rows and columns in the database.

Zachman does not give us a step by step process for creating a new architecture. Zachman doesn't even give us much help in deciding if the future architecture we are creating is the best architecture possible. For that matter, Zachman doesn't even give us an approach to show a need for a future architecture. For these and other issues, we are going to need to look at other methodologies.

### The Open Group Architecture Framework (TOGAF)

The Open Group Architecture Framework is best known by its acronym, TOGAF. TOGAF is owned by The Open Group. TOGAF's view of enterprise architecture is shown in the figure below:

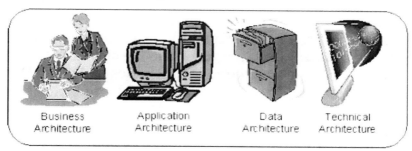

Business Architecture    Application Architecture    Data Architecture    Technical Architecture

*TOGAF Architecture Domain*

As shown in the figure, TOGAF divides an enterprise architecture into four categories, as follows:

- Business architecture—Describes the processes the business uses to meet its goals
- Application architecture—Describes how specific applications are designed and how they interact with each other
- Data architecture—Describes how the enterprise data stores are organized and accessed
- Technical architecture—Describes the hardware and software infrastructure that supports applications and their interactions

TOGAF describes itself as a framework but the most important part of TOGAF is the Architecture Development Method, better known as ADM. ADM is a recipe for creating architecture. A recipe can be categorized as a process. Viewed as an architectural process, TOGAF complements Zachman—which is categorized as an architectural taxonomy. Zachman tells you how to categorize your artifacts. TOGAF gives you a process for creating them. TOGAF views the world of enterprise architecture as a continuum of architectures, ranging from highly generic to highly specific. This continuum is referred as the Enterprise Continuum. It views the process of creating specific enterprise architecture, such as MAM-EA, as moving from the generic to the specific. TOGAF's ADM provides a process for driving this movement from the generic to the specific. TOGAF refers to the most generic architectures as Foundation Architectures. These are architectural principles that can, theoretically, be used by any IT organization in the universe. TOGAF refers to the next specificity level as Industry Architectures. These are principles that one would expect to see in many, but perhaps not all, types of enterprises. TOGAF refers to the next level of specificity Industry Architectures. These are principles that are specific across many enterprises that are part of the same domain. TOGAF calls the most specific level the Organizational Architectures. Figure below shows the relationship between the Enterprise Continuum and the Architecture Development Method (ADM).

TOGAF defines the various knowledge bases that live in the Foundation Architecture. Two that you might run into are the Technical Reference Model (TRM) and the Standards Information Base (SIB). The TRM is a suggested description of a generic IT architecture. The SIB is a collection of standards and pseudo-standards that The Open Group recommends that you consider in building IT architecture. TOGAF presents both the TRM and the SIB as suggestions; though neither is required. TOGAF largely boils down to the Architecture Development Method (ADM). Enterprises will be exposed to the Enterprise Continuum, the SIB, and the TRM. But the day-to-day experience of creating enterprise architecture will be driven by the ADM, a high level view of which is shown in the Figure below.

TOGAF allows phases to be done incompletely, skipped, combined, reordered, or reshaped to fit the needs of the organization.

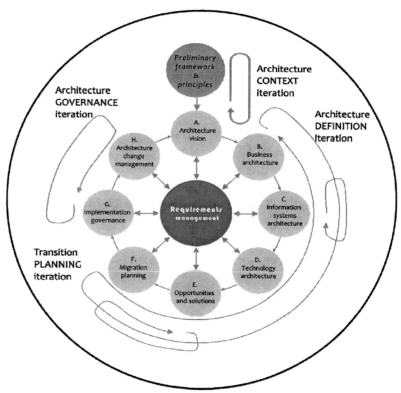

*TOGAF ADM Methodology*

TOGAF is even more flexible about the actual generated architecture. In fact, TOGAF is, to a surprising degree, architecture agnostic. The final architecture might be good, bad, or indifferent. TOGAF merely describes how to generate an enterprise architecture, not necessarily how to generate a good enterprise architecture.

### Federal Enterprise Architecture (FEA)

The Federal Enterprise Architecture (FEA) is the latest attempt by the federal government to unite its myriad agencies and functions under single, common and ubiquitous enterprise architecture. FEA is still in its infancy, as most of the major pieces have been available only since 2006. FEA is the most complete of all the methodologies discussed so far. It has both, a comprehensive taxonomy like Zachman, and an architectural process like TOGAF. FEA can be viewed as either a methodology for creating enterprise architecture or the result of applying that process to a particular enterprise—namely, the U.S. Government.

FEA consists of five reference models, one each for performance: business, service, components, technical, and data. It is true that FEA has these five references models, but there is much more to FEA than just the reference models. A full treatment of FEA needs to include all of the following:

- A perspective on how enterprise architectures should be viewed (the segment model)
- A set of reference models for describing different perspectives of the enterprise
- architecture (the five models, mentioned earlier)
- A process for creating an enterprise architecture
- A transitional process for migrating from a pre-EA to a post-EA paradigm

- A taxonomy for cataloging assets that fall within the purview of the enterprise architecture
- An approach to measuring the success of using the enterprise architecture to drive business

## The FEA Reference Models

The goal of the five FEA reference models is to give standard terms and definitions for the domains of enterprise architecture, and thereby facilitate collaboration and sharing across the federal government. The five reference models in more detail are:

*The Business Reference Model* (BRM) gives a business view of the various functions of the federal government. For example, the BRM defines a standard business capability called water resource management that is a sub-function of natural resources that is considered a line of business of the broader services for citizen's business area.

*The Components Reference Model* (CRM) gives a more IT view of systems that can support business functionality. For example, the CRM defines a customer analytics system described earlier in the hypothetical interchange between the IRS and the GPO.

*The Technical Reference Model* (TRM) defines the various technologies and standards that can be used in building IT systems. For example, the TRM defines HTTP as a protocol that is a subset of a service transport that is a subset of service access and delivery.

*The Data Reference Model* (DRM) defines standard ways of describing data. For example, the DRM defines an entity as something that contains attributes and participates in relationships.

*The Performance Reference Model* (PRM) defines standard ways of describing the value delivered by enterprise architectures. For example, the PRM describes quality as a technology measurement area that is defined as the extent to which technology satisfies functionality or capability requirements.

**The FEA Process**

The FEA Process is primarily focused on creating a segment architecture for a subset of the overall enterprise (in FEA's case, the enterprise is the federal government and the subset is a governmental agency) and is described in the FEA Practice Guidance. The overall segment architecture development process is as follows:

- *Step 1: Architectural Analysis*—Define a simple and concise vision for the segment, and relate it back to the organizational plan.
- *Step 2: Architectural Definition*—Define the desired architectural state of the segment, document the performance goals, consider design alternatives, and develop enterprise architecture for the segment, including business, data, services, and technology architectures.
- *Step 3: Investment and Funding Strategy*— Consider how the project will be funded.
- *Step 4: Program Management Plan and Execute Projects*—Create a plan for managing and executing the project, including milestones and performance measures that will assess project success.

### *Gartner*

Gartner believes that enterprise architecture is about bringing together three constituents: business owners, information specialists and technology implementers. If you can bring these three groups together and unify them behind a common vision that drives business value, you have succeeded. Success is measured in pragmatic terms, such as driving profitability, not by checking off items in a process matrix.

Gartner believes that the enterprise architectures must start with where an organization is going, not with where it is. If we are going to clean house, we don't need to exhaustively document everything we are throwing out. Let's focus our energy on what we want to end up with. As soon as we know our goal, we can see how what we have relates to that goal.

Gartner recommends that an organization begin by telling the story of where its strategic direction is heading and what the business drivers are to which it is responding. Gartner will want this story in plain language, without worrying about prescribed documentation standards, acronyms, or techno babble. The only goal is making sure that everybody understands and shares a single vision.

Most organizations are facing major changes in their business processes. The process of creating an enterprise architecture vision is the organization's opportunity to sit down, take a collective breath, and ensure that everybody understands the nature, the scope, and the impact of those changes. As soon as an organization has this shared vision of the future, it can consider the implications of this vision on the business, technical, information, and solutions architectures of the enterprise. The shared vision of the future will dictate changes in all of these architectures, assign priorities to those changes, and keep those changes grounded in business value.

In the Gartner view enterprise architecture is about strategy, not about engineering. It is focused on the destination. The two things that are most important to Gartner are where an organization is going and how it will get there. Any architectural activity that is extraneous to these questions is irrelevant. Just enough enterprise architecture, just in time, is another way of saying what you will hear from the Gartner analyst.

## *Comparison*

As you can see, the leading enterprise architecture methodologies are very different in their approaches. Which one is best for your organization? There is no one answer to this question. There are 12 criteria used for comparing and evaluating enterprise architectural methodologies (Zachman, TOGAF, FEA, Gartner). Not all of these criteria might be relevant to your organization, and some might be more important than others. But at least these criteria can serve as a starting point for your own evaluation:

- Taxonomy Completeness
- Process Completeness
- Reference Model Guidance
- Practical Guidance
- Maturity Model
- Business Focus
- Governance Guidance
- Partitioning Guidance
- Perspective Catalog
- Vendor Neutrality
- Informative Availability
- Time to Value

At the end of this exercise, you should have a good idea about the strengths and weaknesses of each methodology with respect to your enterprise's needs. If a clear winner emerges, count yourself lucky. Find a consultant who specializes in helping enterprises implement that methodology.

## *Conclusion*

This chapter has covered a broad introduction to the field of enterprise architecture. The history of the field goes back 20 years, but the field is still evolving rapidly. Two of the four major methodologies (Gartner and FEA) have undergone major changes.

These methodologies are quite different from each other, both in goals and in approach. The bad news is that it increases the difficulty for many organizations in choosing one single enterprise architectural methodology. How do you choose between methodologies that have so little in common?

But the good news is that these methodologies can be seen as complementing each other. For many organizations, the best choice is to blend all of these methodologies together in a way that works well within that organization's constraints. This chapter should provide a good starting place for understanding the value of each of these methodologies and how they can complement each other.

# 11. EA Best Practices

This chapter explains best practices, tricks, and techniques for enterprise architecture. They are applicable to both small and large enterprise architecture initiatives, but have special meaning for large ones. The gist of the matter is to have a clear understanding of what one is trying to achieve with enterprise architecture. Organizations will carry out enterprise architecture for one of the following reasons:

- Leverage organization's strategy to gain a competitive advantage
- Rationalize and Modernize information technology that is out of control
- Comply with state and federal regulations

Before we embark on the best practices, here is the list of worst EA practices.

- No Link to Strategic Planning and Budget Process
- Strict Following of EA Frameworks
- Over Standardization
- Analysis Paralysis
- Lack of Business Focus
- Ivory Tower Approach
- Lack of Open Communication
- Lack of a Feedback Loop
- Technology Driving the Architecture
- Technical Talent and Skill Set
- Tools Driving EA
- Focusing on the Current State First or Primarily

### Charter Your EA Programs

The EA program charter represents the agreement between the EA team and the stakeholders.

Program charters are an accepted best practice in most organizations. It is rare to see an enterprise embark on a transformation program (or any other kind of program) without a clearly defined charter that details the expected benefits of the program and the terms of its delivery.

- Development of an EA program charter makes explicit the benefits that the organization expects to achieve with its program and defines how those benefits will be achieved.
- It defines the stakeholders and details their obligations to the EA process.
- It defines the value proposition scope, team organization, vision and risk for the EA.
- It describes the authority of the EA team and explains how decisions will be made.
- It also consists of the timelines for delivery of architecture artefacts and explains how those will be developed.

Over time, the EA program will evolve and the organization's approach to architecture will mature. In addition, the scope of the architecture or the strategic imperatives may also change. So, the charter should be revisited periodically.

### Develop a Communications Plan
Communication is a critical issue for most EA teams, and one that is neglected surprisingly often. For the EA program to be effective, many things must be communicated, including the scope and objectives of the architecture, the decisions that are made (with justifications) and the benefits that are derived from the EA process. When EA teams communicate, they often do so without having developed a formal communications plan. This results in haphazard communications

that are not effective in advancing the EA agenda.
- The key messages must be identified.
- Each stakeholder group must be analyzed to ensure that its specific value proposition is being addressed, and the communication is executed in a way that is effective for that group.
- The messages must be crafted for specific audiences.
- The communications media to be used should be identified.
- An action plan with timelines and responsibilities should be identified.
- A feedback process should be put in place to ensure that the communications plan is effective.

### *Treat Each Iteration like a Project*

EA is not a project with a defined beginning and end and EA teams often neglect project discipline, resulting in an unfocused effort that does not deliver a coherent stream of deliverables. These architecture initiatives are perceived as unprofessional by both the business and the IT community, because they seem to expend effort without any defined goals. It is difficult, if not impossible, to develop an open ended project plan for an entire EA initiative, but it is both possible and desirable to develop project plans for each iteration of the architecture process. In this way, tasks can be planned and resourced, timelines and milestones can be identified and interdependencies can be coordinated. Because enterprise architects often do not make good project managers, successful EA teams often employ professional project managers to ensure that project plans are developed and that project discipline is maintained.

### *Start with the Business Strategy and Obtain Business Sponsorship*

One of the most frequent complaints we hear when we talk to clients is that the business strategy is nonexistent. What is often the case is that the business strategy is not well articulated; it is rarely true that it does not exist. A common error is to confuse the process of developing business strategy—which tends to be complex and involves many factors, such as market research, customer trend analysis and others—with the strategy itself. Business strategy is an articulation of what the company's goals are and what things the company is going to do to achieve those goals. It should not be confused with the studies that are done and the assumptions that are made to achieve that articulation.

In its simplest form, the business strategy consists of the answers to five simple questions.

- What does the company want to do?
- Who is (are) the target market(s) for the goods and services that the company provides?
- What is the geographic scope of the strategy?
- What is the time frame in which goals should be accomplished?
- How to accomplish these goals?

One good place to look for your business strategy is on the investor relations portion of your company's Web site. People are not anxious to invest in a company that does not have clearly stated goals and an action plan for strategy.

### *Be Pragmatic*

One of the common mistakes we see EA teams make is attempt to produce comprehensive enterprise architecture as their first deliverable. They get bogged down trying to model the entire enterprise and as a result produce little or nothing of immediate value, and languish as the enterprise loses interest and moves on.

A more effective approach is to choose pragmatic targets based on the strategic imperatives of the enterprise. In this way you can concentrate on issues that are truly important to the business and deliver value quickly before the organization loses interest. What is not modeled in this iteration will be modeled in the next one or in the iteration after that. By maintaining focus on modeling the current strategic imperatives, you will ensure that the critical issues that are important to the enterprise are the ones being addressed.

### EA Governance

Governance is defined as the process of making decisions and setting the chain of commands. There are two kinds of EA governance: – governance around the making of architectural decisions, and governance as architecture assurance. These two types of governance serve different purposes and very often require different organizational structures and formats. The most effective architecture programs are the ones that ensure a wide range of participants in both types of governance. EA teams that include implementation experts in the lower level architectural decisions find that they encounter less resistance to EA standards on the part of implementation teams. Because the designers and implementers have a hand in making architectural decisions, they feel they have ownership of the architecture rather than architecture being viewed as externally imposed constraints.

Similarly, architecture teams that include business participation in the architecture assurance process typically see higher levels of business sponsorship, which is critical to the success of the EA initiative.

146

An important point to remember is that no EA is comprehensive enough to anticipate every possible business requirement that might come up in the future and there will always be a good business reason to make exceptions. A formal process for making exceptions is critical.

### Agile Methodology

An Agile method is a way to build software using the small optimized revisions that resemble the iterative and incremental approach. The key element of an Agile method is that it ensures that the risk elements are kept at bay. Earlier methodologies have galvanized into the Agile and Agile is a reflection of its predecessor's best practices. In the Scrum method of Agile software development, work is confined to a regular, repeatable work cycle, known as a *sprint* or iteration. Scrum sprints used to be 30 days long, but today many teams prefer shorter sprints, such as one-week or two-week sprints.

One sprint would contain analysis, design, development, testing, and deployment. This sprint would form one delivery, e.g., 1.0.1. The next sprint would be delivery 1.0.2 and so on and so forth. There would be multiple such sprints spanning the entire product life cycle from inception phase until the end of the product life span. The following diagram depicts Agile at the core.

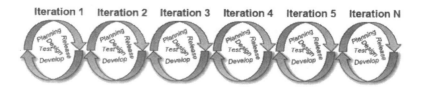

The table below compares the Agile Vs Traditional approach:

| Agile | Traditional |
|---|---|
| Incremental Value & Risk Management | Phased approach with an attempt to know everything at the start |
| Embracing Change | Repelling Change |
| Delivery Early, Fail Early | Delivers value at the end, fails at the end |
| Transparency | Detailed planning, stagnant control |
| Inspect and Adapt | Meta Solution w/tightly controlled procedures & final answers |
| Self-Managed | Command and Control |
| Continual Learning | Learning is secondary to the pressure of delivery |

*Agile Vs Traditional*

## Architectural Decisions

Architectural decisions become an effective tool to help stakeholders understand the architecture. These decisions can provide a concrete direction for implementation and serve as an effective tool for communication to customers and management.

148

A complex architecture probably reflects thousands of decisions. Is it necessary for an architect to make and explicitly document all of them? An architect absolutely should make the decisions that identify the system's key structural elements, their externally visible properties, and their relationships. To test a decision's architectural significance, an architect should ask the following question: *Does this decision affect one or more system qualities (performance, availability, modifiability, security, and so on)? If so, an architect should make a decision.*

Properly documenting architectural decisions is critical because architects make them in complex environments and they involve tradeoffs. A simple document describing key architecture decisions can go a long way in demystifying past and future system architectures. Once the team reaches a final architectural decision, they'll need to communicate the results to convince the rest of the organization that they've chosen appropriately. The architectural decision template is useful because it provides a common language for discussing decisions. Reviewers can easily see the decision's status, rationale, and impacts. In practice, this has proven to be much more powerful than reviewing; e.g., component models. The team should communicate controversial decisions early and often and undisputed decisions during the normal review process.

| Name | Description |
|---|---|
| Issue | Design issue that is getting addressed |
| Decision | The architecture decision |
| Status | The status i.e. pending, decided or approved |
| Layer/Component | The layer such as integration, presentation or data |
| Assumption | This states the underlying assumptions i.e. cost, schedule, technology |
| Constraint | Captures the additional constraints in the environment |
| Options | List of options that are considered |
| Implications | This is the implication around the architecture decision |
| Related Requirement | This maps to the requirement or the business objective |
| Notes | Useful to capture notes that the team discuss during the socialization process |

*Architectural Decision Template*

### *Measuring the Value Delivered by EA*

To effectively demonstrate the value of EA the concerns of individual stakeholders must be recognized, and the measures that demonstrate progress against those concerns must be worked out. The EA value proposition will be different in organizations with different business strategies, different industries, different cultures and different levels of maturity. There is no standard set of measures that apply. A common problem is architecture teams are called on to justify after the effort. Because they don't have any measurement in place that can demonstrate the value of what they are doing, they are forced to rely on subjective evidence.

High performing enterprise architecture teams define value proposition, and identify appropriate measures to demonstrate that value proposition as part of the preparation work for an EA iteration. Then they measure and report on a regular basis.

### *Track EA Program Maturity*

One of the interesting phenomena is the architecture programs that start out being very effective, become less effective over time. As enterprise adopts the strategic discipline of enterprise architecture it becomes more mature and sophisticated over time. If the architecture program does not change, a point will be reached where the enterprise has moved beyond the capability of the EA program to provide benefit.

Best practice EA teams treat their programs as processes that must continually improve over time. That means, evaluating the current level of maturity on a regular basis setting realistic goals for the next evaluation cycle, analyzing the critical constraints that prevent the program from being as effective as it should be and developing concrete action plans to address those constraints.

Measure your EA program maturity regularly (once a year) as part of a program of continuous improvement. Set realistic targets for improvement and carefully analyze the constraints that impede your effectiveness.

151

## Enterprise Architects Competencies

Members of the core architecture team require a common set of talents that enable effective participation in the development of the architecture. The talents that are required by architects are rare in IT professionals, adding to the difficulty in recruiting the architecture team. Specifically, architects must have a talent for:

- *Conceptualization:* Visualizing the solution, process or infrastructure that is required
- *Innovation:* Exploring new opportunities that add to the business value proposition or reduce costs
- *Enterprise Perspective:* Understanding the broader implications of strategy across all business units
- *Foresight:* Wrestling the short, medium and long-term planning horizons
- *Consensus building:* Enabling a group of people with diverse backgrounds to accept majority or common conclusion
- *Facilitation:* Guiding a debate without dominating the conclusion
- *Leadership:* Influencing a broad audience to adopt a particular path
- *Logic:* Selecting the best solution from a range of options to resolve an issue or seize an opportunity
- *Communication:* Effectively convey the results of the architecture, the process to develop it and the value it provides

## Architectural Alternatives

The general guidance is to provide up to three options or alternatives for a solution. This is generally applicable to solution or application architectures. The recommendation is generally made in terms of which is the best solution based on the suitability and several other factors influencing the solution. This typically applies to application architecture where the options are included based on different vendor products and a table listening pros and cons is also created including the benefits of the alternatives.

### Enterprise Architecture Myths and Facts

The following diagram depicts myths and reality about enterprise architecture.

| Myths |
|---|
| Re-architecting the enterprise systems |
| Only about Frameworks- Zachman |
| Designing applications using J2EE, .Net, or similar |
| Method to organize Enterprise Data to facilitate integration |
| Method to Design IT Systems |
| A one time event |

| Reality |
|---|
| Is "Enterprise" Architecture |
| Involves overall documentation & management of all aspects of Enterprise |
| Is a Business & IT issue, not just an IT issue |
| Has nothing to do with Java or .Net but enterprise application landscape in totality |
| Is not the silver-bullet to solve all the IT problems |
| Is a Journey |

*EA Myths & Facts*

### Summary

## Benefits to Business

When an EA program is performing well, the benefits are apparent to a wide range of stakeholders. The business gains better alignment of IT and business strategy, bringing with it a host of benefits, including decreased time to market and cost, business agility, a better return on technology investments and better all-around information for decision making.

In today's competitive climate, resources must be carefully allocated in a way that provides the most business value and the flexibility to respond to changes in the markets. The competitive landscape and the regulatory climate is the key and the ability of the EA team to work proactively with the business to develop a vision can mean the difference between success and failure. As best practice EA programs mature, EA and IT become true strategic partners in the development of a business strategy, allowing the business to achieve true competitive differentiation through well designed and streamlined processes, data and technology.

**Benefits to IT**

When the IT organization adopts a strategic planning and best practice approach to the acquisition and operation of technology assets, the benefits are wide ranging. The operational environment is more stable. For instance, when less money is spent to keep the lights on, there is more money to spend on innovation that can bring greater competitive advantage. Projects are less costly and less risky, more of them are completed on time and within budget, and more of them actually deliver the value that was promised when they were proposed. The business looks at the IT organization as a partner in achieving the strategic direction of the business rather than just an annoying cost center. When IT's mission is aligned with fulfilling the business' mission, the entity is transformed into an agile enterprise.

154

# 12. Conclusion

Making the leap from technology centric architecture to business centric architecture might be enterprise architect's biggest challenge yet. Business architecture is not simply another enterprise architecture (EA) view. It is an entirely different way to think about architecture with its own set of goals, processes, and deliverables. Though the shift to business technology will be difficult, the rewards will be great. Business architecture will provide the major vehicle for aligning IT capabilities with business outcomes. Well defined business architecture will provide new business insights, uncover unseen opportunities, and guide business investments to where they deliver the most value. CIOs will want to direct their enterprise architects to sharpen their business skills, increase their business interactions, and develop their business architecture road map.

### Traditional EA Paradigm is Evolving

Enterprise architecture's long standing paradigm of driving cost savings from the bottom of the technology stack is changing. CIOs and business leaders are looking for large scale efficiencies through outsourcing, offshoring, and Software as a Service (SaaS). Architects who work at an engineering level are now finding that their influence is waning. And while cost saving is still important, business executives now want IT to deliver more creative products that can help drive sales and increase revenue. These shifts are driving new challenges for architects.

*Influence over technology is shrinking.* IT leaders are showing an increased willingness to look outside their organizations to lower costs and reduce operational complexity. Outsourcing infrastructure, offshoring development tasks, and purchasing application packages are all growing trends. The current economic conditions will drive even more interest in finding less expensive alternatives to build and run business systems. Why are business and IT leaders willing to make these changes? Because, their views is changing about the role IT plays are changing. IT Organizations outsource their infrastructure when they believe it offers no competitive advantage. Development organizations offshore programming when they conclude that writing code is a commodity, and business analysis, design and architecture are the added value. IT's "buy before build" strategy encourages the business view of IT as a provider of services, not a creator of services.

*Competition for business architecture leadership is heating up.* Enterprise architects have rarely had to compete for their role. Other organizational players who focused on business or technology silos are happy to let EA deal with the complex inter-organizational and cross technology domain issues. Business architecture, however, is drawing interest from a variety of areas. Business analysts are taking a bottom-up approach and presenting process models as a component of business architecture. Leading edge business thinkers are working top down to create an actionable view of business capabilities and the business model. Both IT and business strategists are beginning to use the business architecture labels to describe their deliverables. In this environment, traditional architects will struggle to even maintain a seat at the table, much less control.

*EA has become typecast as an IT focused discipline.* The roots of modern enterprise architecture can be traced back to John Zachman's publication of "A Framework for Information Systems Architecture" in

1987. Five years later, Steven Spewak published the first EA book, *Enterprise Architecture Planning*. Shortly thereafter, in 1997, The Open Group published TOGAF 1.0, the first EA development methodology, and in 1999, the US Federal CIO Council developed the Federal Enterprise Architecture Framework to guide US government agencies in the application of technology. The period between 1987 and 2000 can be seen as the golden age of EA, that created the foundation for much of the current day EA approaches. EA development has clearly slowed down since 2000. The original models have been enhanced and extended, but little has been added in the way of new concepts and constructs. The current EA models do not address the business need for IT's participation in value creation and business innovation.

### *EA should be more Business Focused*

A business centric architecture looks very different from a technology centric architecture. Business artifacts are designed more to spur thinking and provide insight than to standardize decisions. Coherence is much less important than illumination. Collaboration and influence replace governance. To create a business centric architecture, architects will have to create new models rather than extend old ones.

*Increase their focus on the business elements of EA.* Enterprise architecture teams are resource constrained. There is more work to do in the technology domain than most teams can accomplish. Until EA can demonstrate a business architecture value proposition, it will have to use the resources it has. This means redirecting attention from the never ending stream of technical work to new areas with more business focus.

*Create new business tools.* Traditional EA tools will not expand well into the business space. Architects will have to learn the tools business leaders know and understand, as well as create a few new ones. Basic business tools to work at a business strategy level are value chains, supply chains, strategy maps, Balanced Scorecards, SWOT analyses, and value streams. Businesses may be less familiar with using tools such as business models and business capability maps. Business architects will have to educate business leaders on the value of these and other new tools.

*Develop new business skills.* Architecture teams are largely made up of super technologists. Their deep understanding of technology and their problem solving skills brought them credibility and acceptance in the early years of EA. Over time, architects grew their skills beyond solving yesterday's problems to designing better solutions for the future. Savvy architects leveraged these skills to move even further up the project process chain to provide analysis and insight IT investments. But now, the business is looking for something different from IT. Business leaders expect IT to help create new business value. If architects want to play a leading role in this shift, they will have to become more business savvy. They will have to move beyond seeing the business as a collection of processes to understanding fundamental business drivers such as competitive positioning, globalized marketplaces, and business model innovation.

| | Technology Centric Architecture | Business Centric Architecture |
|---|---|---|
| **Focus** | Technology Standards | Business Strategy |
| | Technology Portfolio | Business Capability, Operating Models & Value Chain |
| | Architecture Patterns | |
| | | Application & Information from Business Process Perspectives |
| | Application & Information architectures | |
| | | Business Investment Governance |
| **Tools** | Technical Domain Maps | Value Chains, Supply Chain, SWOT, Strategy Maps, Value Streams, Business Capability Maps |
| | Architecture Patterns | |
| | Project Reviews | |
| **Architect Skills** | Top Technologist SME for Application and Infrastructure teams | Business Advisors SME for linking business needs to IT capabilities & Services |

*Business Vs Technology Centric Architecture*

## *Important Trends in EA*

- What are the hottest trends that enterprise architects and IT managers need to watch over the next two to three years?

- **Next generation BI takes shape, combining real time access with pervasiveness, agility, and self-service:** "Firms will increase their use of analytics to improve their speed of response to changing market conditions ... IT needs to enable successful end user BI self-service to keep runaway BI costs in check."

- **Business rules processing and policy-based SOA move to the mainstream:** "Business rules processing automates highly conditional transactions that staff members perform manually. Both business rules and policy-based SOA will be important for applications that are 'built for change.'"

- **SaaS and cloud based platforms become standard:** "Even if IT mostly uses IaaS and PaaS options, the business will benefit from rapid deployment. IT execs must triage where they invest

159

their resources, as well as adopt new application support practices for SaaS, while completely re-evaluating capacity issues as well as architecture standards for applications developed or hosted in the cloud."

- **System management enables continued virtualization** (new trend): "IT must acquire and deploy comprehensive management tools, obtain training, and gain some experience in these tools before coming anywhere near mastery. Utilization of vendors' service offerings will spike."

- **Collaboration platforms become people centric:** "Communication and collaboration technologies converge, leading to greater organizational responsiveness to business changes."

- **Event driven patterns demand attention** (new trend): Event processing has the potential for significant business impact; complexity and IT's lack of experience in this area will somewhat limit progress. Architects and developers will need to understand when to handle events with custom code, business rules, or CEP platforms and adapt event processing mindsets to their SOA environments."

- **Customer community platforms integrate with business apps:** "Some firms and functions within the firms will take advantage of this and learn how to use the insights from customer communities to produce better products and services, heighten market visibility, and lower costs."

- **Apps and business processes go mobile on powerful devices and faster networks:** "Business processes will be extended to the mobile workforce, bringing greater efficiency and compliance. IT must add mobile support to applications and will be challenged to manage and secure mobile devices and networks."

- **Analytics target text and social networks** (new trend): "These new technologies bring powerful analytics to bear on rich areas as yet untapped for intelligence about customers and products. They will provide a challenge for information architects and tax the semantic capabilities of existing investments."
- **IaaS finds a broader audience** (new trend): "IaaS provides agility and flexibility for enabling high impact areas such as MDM and BI. IaaS can significantly alter IT's approach to its data management strategy."

### *Qualities for Enterprise Architects*

Regardless of what domain or scope they work in, there are a common set of skills that all architects have. While architecture at the enterprise scope is required to create the big picture view and provide context, the value of architecture comes when it is applied to help and influence projects. So let's look at 10 things an architect does in the context of a typical project lifecycle.

- *Inquire:* Architects are asked to solve specific problems. Getting to the core of the problem and soliciting requirements is the first step in addressing any given set of requirements. Of course, the requirements are often vague and presented in the limited focus of a specific application domain. So the inquiry must solicit specific requirements and goals, as well as an understanding of how those requirements fit into the broader enterprise context.
- *Integrate:* Architects act as a bridge between a given project or solution and how that project fits into

161

the broader context. One of the major benefits that an architect brings to the enterprise is integrating the solution for the particular project with the business domain, enterprise concerns, industry standards, established patterns, and best practices.

- *Analyze:* Architects have to analyze the information that they have collected. The analysis consists of answering three architectural questions: (1) What are the key elements of the problem or solution? (2) What are the relationships between them? and (3) How do they combine together to provide higher value.

- *Conceptualize:* Once the overall, integrated solution is framed, the architect needs to create a conceptual vision of the solution. This will typically be in the form of a conceptual architecture diagram, a drawing that shows the major users/channels of the system, the other systems it has to interact with, and the major logical functions and data that it must perform or use. It also must establish the scope of the project within those pieces.

- *Abstract:* The architect also has to communicate the key details to many audiences. This can be accomplished through the use of architectural viewpoints, such as business, information, application, and technology perspectives. Abstraction can be defined as the suppression of irrelevant detail. So one key abstraction is to apply separation of concerns (filters) to establish what details are, and are not, important for that viewpoint. Within each perspective, the viewpoint will also be presented in different levels of abstraction, often referred to as conceptual, logical, and physical architectures.

- *Visualize:* They say a picture is worth a thousand words. It is also an excellent way to represent the architectural models and drawings at each level of abstraction. So another key skill and function of the architect is to create visual renditions of the different abstractions and viewpoints.

- *Formalize:* Of course, architecture needs to be more than just pretty pictures. It needs to be specific enough to unambiguously communicate the details to whoever is going to implement the architecture. An architectural "specification" is the usual approach to formalization. But the specification does not have to be a document. A visualization in the form of a complete and precise formal model, expressed in industry standard notation, is often more beneficial.

- *Communicate:* This is probably the single most important aspect of an architect's job. Fundamentally, architects are in the role of communicator. After they establish and formalize a solution, they need to communicate that solution as well as its importance and value to stakeholders throughout the organization.

- *Enable:* Even the best designed, formalized, and communicated architecture may not be successful. The equation for architecture value is actually pretty straightforward. If uing architecture will make someone's job easier, they'll use it. If it adds extra steps and work, without adding extra value, it will be ignored. Of course, achieving this goal is anything but simple, but a key to achieving architecture's goal of influencing IT projects and systems depends on the extent to which architects enable the target audience to easily use the architecture.

- *Assist:* Finally, one of the primary enablers for architecture is to actively assist projects in using it. This is the single most important activity architects can do to make their architecture real. Virtually all successful architecture programs include some aspect of consulting to projects.

## Summary

The transformation from technical architecture to business architecture will be neither easy nor fast. The good news is that architects can move business architecture initiatives forward with little investment or top down support. Five practical, doable steps architecture teams can take to build business centric architecture practices are:

*Build business IQ.* Architects have deep technical skills and expend most of their discretionary time and money enhancing their already significant technical knowledge rather than branching out into developing their leadership and business acumen. Successful architects in the future must be business-savvy. Don't have the time? Think again. The average business book is shorter than 300 pages.

*Cultivate business mentors.* Business executives understand the power of one-on-one mentoring relationships. Many companies have formal mentoring programs to help jump-start up and coming business leaders. A mentor in the business can provide guidance on experiential learning opportunities and open the door to other business leaders who can expand your perspective. Mentors give architects support and advice on executive level presentations and putting together successful funding requests. Most importantly, a business mentor will provide insight about your company's management and business practices that just can't be attained any other way.

*Design architecture for your business consumers.* Abstract notions about providing enterprise value lead to abstract solutions that are hard to communicate and even harder to connect to business realities. Creating an EA practice focused on the EA consumer ensures a business aligned architecture. Who are EA's consumers? They are the people who interact directly with architects and their products.

*Create a business architecture for IT.* Business architecture is more than a simple extension of current EA views into the business. Extending current EA models to create a business architecture will result in an IT centric view of the business as opposed to the desired business centric view of IT. Architects can develop their business architecture tool kit and hone their business skills by starting with what they know best. With your CIO, identify a challenge or set of challenges in "running IT as a business." Select and create the business architecture deliverables that provide insights for addressing these challenges. Use this working model to sell the concept to IT relationship managers. Now you have the tools and skills necessary to promote business architecture to the business.

*Rethink the current EA paradigm.* EA leaders should regularly take a step back and assess the EA practice's current activities and direction to ensure it is moving toward high impact activities and not devolving into a pool of great technical resources. EA leaders should be able to clearly answer the following questions:

1) "Are we creating insight and strategy, or are we engineering systems?"

2) "Are we attempting to control others through governance and policy, or are we working to influence leadership thinking?"

3) "Are we focused on architecture purity and coherence or on delivering value?"

4) "Are we promising future benefits or providing real value in real time?"

5) "Are we making technology decisions for the business, or are we making business decisions about technology?"

In the immortal words of the Yogi Berra, "The future ain't what it used to be." The future of enterprise architecture will not be a simple extension of current EA models into the business domain. Technology centric architecture is all about what is. Business architecture is about what could be. Architects will have to learn new skills, new tools, new techniques, and a whole new mindset if they want to lead their company's business architecture initiative. The road to the future is a long journey. Better get started!

# Index

# About the Authors

**Dr. Gopala Krishna Behara** is an Enterprise Architect with 19+ years of extensive experience in the ICT industry that spans across Pre-Sales, Consulting, Enterprise Architecture, Service Oriented Architecture, Business Process Management, Solution Architecture, Project Management, Product Development and Systems Integration. He is certified in Open Group TOGAF, and IBM Cloud Solutions. He serves as an Advisory Architect and Mentor on Enterprise Architecture, Application Portfolio Rationalization and Architecture Assurance initiatives and continues to work as a Subject Matter Expert and Author. He has worked on multiple architecture transformation engagements in the USA, UK, Europe, Asia Pacific and Middle East Regions that presented a phased roadmap to transformation that maximized the business value, while minimizing costs and risks.

Dr.Gopal is currently working as a Senior Enterprise Architect in the Global Enterprise Architecture group of Wipro. He has published White Papers in International Journals in SOA, BPM & e-Governance spaces and also made a significant contribution to the SOA Reference Architecture definition.

**Sameer S. Paradkar** is an Enterprise Architect with 15+ years of experience in the ICT industry which spans across Consulting, Product Development and Systems Integration. He is an Open Group TOGAF, Oracle Master Java EA, TMForum NGOSS, IBM SOA Solutions, IBM Cloud Solutions, IBM MobileFirst and ITIL Foundation V3 certified architect. He serves as an advisory architect on Enterprise Architecture initiatives and continues to work as a Subject Matter Expert. He has worked on multiple architecture transformation engagements in the USA, UK, Europe, Asia Pacific and Middle East Regions that presented a phased roadmap to transformation that maximized the business value, while minimizing costs and risks.

Sameer specializes in IT Strategies and Enterprise transformation engagements and currently is part of IT Strategy & Transformation Practice in AtoS. Prior to AtoS, he worked in organizations like EY - IT Advisory, IBM GBS, Wipro Consulting Services, TechMahindra and Infosys Technologies.

# Review Team

We would to thank following team members for providing feedback and valuable inputs for the book:

**Ajay Shendye**, Principal Solution Architect, IT Strategy & Transformation, AtoS

**Amarendra Nargundkar**, IT Strategy and Governance Consultant, TCS

**Awadhesh Kumar**, Enterprise Architect, IT Strategy & Transformation, AtoS

**Nitin Bhandarkar**, Principal Architect, IT Strategy & Transformation, AtoS

**Rajesh Ghosh**, Principal Architect, IT Strategy & Transformation, AtoS

**Shib Rath**, Management Consultant/Program Manager, Hewlett-Packard

**Shrinath Rao**, Senior Architect, IT Strategy & Transformation, AtoS

**Subhankar Ghosh**, Practice Head, IT Strategy & Transformation, AtoS

**Sudhanshu Saxena**, Principal Architect, IT Strategy & Transformation, AtoS

**Vikash Kumar**, Senior Architect, IT Strategy & Transformation, AtoS

**Hari Kishan Burle**, Vice President, Global Enterprise Architecture, Wipro Technologies

**Raju Alluri,** Global Delivery Head, Global Enterprise Architecture, Wipro Technologies

**Prasad Palli**, Lead Enterprise Architect, Global Enterprise Architecture, Wipro Technologies

**Disclaimer**

The views expressed in title are that of the authors and organizations do not subscribe to the substance, veracity or truthfulness of the said opinion.

# Companion Books

**Cognitive Computing**
A Brief Guide for Game Changers

**The Cognitive Enterprise**

**Business Architecture**
The Art and Practice of Business Transformation

**Dot Cloud**
The 21st Century business Platform Built on Cloud Computing

**Business Innovation in the Cloud**
Strategies for Executing on Innovation with Cloud Computing

**Value Networks**
And the True Nature of Collaboration

**Smart Process Apps**
The Next Breakout Business Advantage

**Human Interactions**
The Heart and Soul of Business Process Management

**Enterprise Cloud Computing**
A Strategy Guide for Business and Technology Leaders

**Extreme Competition**
Innovation and the Great 21st Century Business Reformation

**Business Process Management**
The Third Wave

**Business Process Management**
The Next Wave

**Mastering the Unpredictable**
How Adaptive Case Management Will Revolutionize
the Way That Knowledge Workers Get Things Done

See more at...

www.mkpress.com
*Innovation at the Intersection of Business and Technology*

CPSIA information can be obtained
at www.ICGtesting.com
Printed in the USA
LVOW10s0232301117
558119LV00011B/25/P